T0171645

The Art of
Natural Leadership

Rhoda Kreuzer

WESTBOW
PRESS
A DIVISION OF THOMAS NELSON

WestBow Press books may be ordered through booksellers or by contacting:

WestBow Press
A Division of Thomas Nelson
1663 Liberty Drive
Bloomington, IN 47403
www.westbowpress.com
1-(866) 928-1240

Because of the dynamic nature of the Internet, any web addresses or links contained in this book may have changed since publication and may no longer be valid. The views expressed in this work are solely those of the author and do not necessarily reflect the views of the publisher, and the publisher hereby disclaims any responsibility for them.

Any people depicted in stock imagery provided by Thinkstock are models, and such images are being used for illustrative purposes only.

Certain stock imagery © Thinkstock.

ISBN: 978-1-4497-3167-0 (sc)
ISBN: 978-1-4497-3168-7 (hc)
ISBN: 978-1-4497-3166-3 (e)

Library of Congress Control Number: 2011960568

Printed in the United States of America

WestBow Press rev. date: 1/19/2012

Table of Contents

Notes of Thanks

This book could not have been realized without the support and input of many people. My deepest thanks to my mother, who modeled true leadership and has always encouraged and supported me. Thanks to my husband, Eric Kreuzer, and our son, Rick, for believing that I could accomplish this undertaking even though the task seemed daunting. Their support and continued belief in me was invaluable in completing this project.

Many thanks to the leaders in my life and community who have been role models for myself and others, including John Karle from Crosby & Henry; Mike Verhulst from Summit Landscape; my CEO Round Table members; and the many others who are identified throughout this book. Without these bright and shining examples, our world would not be what it is today.

Author's Notes

There are many books about leadership, and some would ask, why write another? For years, I resisted people's suggestions to write a book, until I realized a paradigm so strong, so impactful, that I knew I had to share it. In particular, I began to see connections between corporate culture and "natural" leadership as well as the lessons we can all learn from the natural world, which gives us such key concepts as sustainability, ecosystems, and competition. I therefore created an "environmental" paradigm of the corporate world that has great strength for teaching leaders what it means to serve with excellence. This "natural" theme has become the central metaphor for my lessons on leadership; I will make analogies between situations in the natural world and the corporate environment, will use terms such as "natural leaders" to refer to those who understand and make use of these connections, and will even introduce my friendly environmental steward, Ned, to explain my lessons. Throughout, I'll emphasize that "natural" leaders are not born; they are made.

Therefore, this is not just another leadership book; rather, it is a crucial, proven guide for leaders everywhere. Within are the keys that will propel you to excellence in leadership, organizational growth, and a legacy that goes beyond momentary profitability. It is my hope that you will glean gold nuggets to propel you on your journey to becoming a courageous and strong leader.

Introduction:

Crisis and legacy

I t is important to recognize that the corporate world is experiencing a crisis of leadership. In fact, to understand the magnitude of the problem, it's useful to compare it to the current environmental crisis in the natural world.

So let's look at the current state of our natural environment. It's become clear to most of us that our responsibility as humans has always been to live in harmony with nature and take care of our planet. And yet the world's leaders, until recent years, have shut their eyes to that task and instead invested in short-term gains. They have squandered resources today, creating a heavy burden for many generations to come. As scientists learn more about the interconnectedness of nature, one thing is very clear: we are depleting natural resources and losing opportunities to sustain a healthy, thriving environment. A world that was once full of promise and life is quickly becoming dismal and lackluster.

However, there is a bright prospect on the horizon. Leaders around the world are beginning to learn about an array of environmental concerns and are responding positively to those needs. For instance, as freshwater supplies become contaminated or greatly diminished, leaders are faced with making decisions about where to get water. In response, legislators are now taking positive steps to create laws to protect our water supplies, while community leaders are creating methods to reduce water use and control the contaminants that enter our water sources. They are working to avoid the predictions of experts who have estimated that in a matter of fifty years, purchasing drinking water will be a major budget item in every household. Thus, leaders who take their responsibilities seriously to protect and save the environment are thereby serving the constituents who have elected them.

The issues and needs represented in the "green" or environmental movement reflect the issues faced by corporate leaders. In the business world, as in our larger environment, leadership is not optional, but rather a necessity. Without effective leadership, organizations will crumble and fall. Regardless of circumstances, people must have a strong leader to follow. Depending on the strengths of leaders, organizations will either grow and reach their goals or decline. While the thrust of this book will discuss the concept of leadership in the workplace, the same concepts and principles are true for any other area of life as well. There is no such thing as an organization or family without a leader. There are only organizations with either poor or strong leaders.

In researching and studying leaders and their characteristics, I've discovered three areas of mastery that allow them to be strong and effective. Take any of these three masteries away, and the rest crumbles. Each of these areas seems very simple, and in theory, they are. However, in practice they're extremely difficult to implement. This difficulty is increased by the fact that we must resist our own culture, which pulls us *away* from the three areas that will allow us to reach our goals and our full leadership potential. Those three masteries include:

- Mastery of self: The capacity to discipline, focus, and control your natural impulses.
- Mastery of purpose: The capacity to create mission and inspire others to great achievements.
- Mastery of team: The capacity to identify, motivate, and lead a team of people committed to the same purpose.

All three of these masteries are critical. From them arise great leaders, great teams, and great achievements. None of these can be replaced by technical expertise, by luck, or by financial astuteness. These three masteries, throughout history, have been the hallmarks of all great movements and leaders.

You will also discover an order to these masteries. Many leaders try to jump ahead and master their team skills without first mastering themselves. Entrepreneurs are often more attracted by the activity and tangible aspects of mastering the team. They tend to resist the more difficult self-reflection involved in mastering themselves. Such an approach will not work. You must first master yourself, then your purpose and passion, and then your team-building skills. In this way, you create a solid foundation on which the others rest.

When these masteries are neglected, we witness disengagement, frustration, and the longing for something better. In the United States, for example, some organizations have a turnover rate of 100 percent a year! These companies have teams that are frustrated with management's inability to lead and provide a meaningful place in which to achieve success. Leaders in these organizations talk about a vision for their company but fail to connect it to their teams' initiatives. Their employees will leave and seek a more vibrant future elsewhere. Many employees desire opportunities to be engaged, to contribute in meaningful ways, and to work together for something that is worthwhile and impactful.

However, most leaders choose to follow the same paths as their predecessors. They are creating "ecosystems" (cultures) that are sick, lethargic, and full of pollutants. They attract people with great promises and large salaries, only to lose them once their employees realize that the culture and environment is fraudulent. It's like spraying industrial-sized cans of air freshener next to a wastewater treatment plant; the smell might disappear for a brief time, but then the spray dissipates and the strong odor returns. You can remodel your office, create a new logo and tagline, and promise anything you wish. But those promises will only last for a short time before people recognize the truth: your company's leadership is bankrupt, the culture is corrosive, and your promises are empty. Such a corporate ecosystem cannot sustain itself and will inevitably decay.

We can better understand this concept of sustainable corporate ecosystems, or cultures, when we borrow the term "carbon footprint" from the environmental movement. Environmentalists use this term to describe the negative impact that humans leave on our world when they deplete natural resources. Our impact can be seen in the stripping away of forest areas, the contamination of water, and the extinction of wildlife. We are using a large percent of the natural resources in the world, but we are not replenishing them. Thus, we are creating environmental issues that will take decades to reverse.

Just as carbon footprints leave a mark on our environment, corporate leaders leave a carbon footprint on their business spheres. Leaders leave unique imprints that demonstrate their values, character, philosophy, and vision, thereby shaping the culture of an organization. Just as we cannot take a plane, drive a car, or turn on a light bulb without leaving a carbon footprint, leaders cannot help but leave their marks on their organizations. The only question for leaders is whether they'll leave a positive legacy or a negative burden.

In particular, strong, positive leaders have a tremendous impact on whether corporate culture is healthy and rich or drains resources. For better or worse, a workplace culture or environment will either cause us to thrive or erode the vitality of our team. Therefore, leaders must hold themselves accountable for the way in which they lead and for the carbon footprint they leave. Only strong, positive leadership will create healthy, thriving organizations.

Likewise, your talent pool, profitability, and productivity are all statistically based on your leadership ability.[1] Natural leaders excel in these areas and create excellence wherever they go. No leader or organization is perfect, but natural leaders are always striving to grow and improve. They understand their personal responsibility in shaping the vision and culture of their organization and preparing their team for sustainable success.

Through reading this book, you will discover a better way to lead and leave a true legacy as you follow the tenets of the natural leader. You will be re-energized by the journey and rediscover the joy of leading others to great achievements. In addition, you will create greater meaning, purpose, and impact in choosing to serve others. Welcome to the world of natural leadership!

---

1   Marcus Buckingham and Curt Coffman, *First, Break All the Rules: What the World's Greatest Managers Do Differently* (New York: Simon and Schuster, 1999).

Part I:
Mastery of Self

Chapter 1:

Integrity

The young man reached for the latch on the garden gate, but then he paused. Could this organization really be as good as they said? Would he really find a harmonious and vibrant environment cared for by strong leaders?

He forced himself to open the gate. It creaked just slightly, and then through the opening he saw something he could hardly take in. It was more than a mere garden; it was an entire ecosystem that was so bright, so green, so vibrant that it was almost blinding. There was nothing to compare it to, nothing that came close to anything he had seen before.

Everywhere he looked, there were peaceful, awe-inspiring scenes. He was surrounded by lush flora, waterfalls the color of blue glass, birds chirping gleefully, fragrant flowers, and clear, crisp air. It felt like a fairy tale come true. Where was he? How could such a wonderful, lush, vibrant ecosystem exist?

He stepped through the door, drinking in the beautiful scenery around him. As he wandered through the delightful landscape, he heard a noise over to the left. There he saw a man who was bent over a plant, inspecting the leaves. The gardener was so intent on his work that he didn't notice the young man's presence. He seemed interested only in what he was doing.

"Excuse me, sir. I'm Adam," said the young man. The older man didn't look up or turn, but just kept working on the plant. "Excuse me," Adam said again, clearing his throat. "I believe we had an appointment? I'm here to shadow you and learn from you. Sorry I'm a bit early." The gardener's only acknowledgement was to lift his hand, signaling Adam to wait just a moment. Finally, he seemed satisfied with what he had accomplished and slowly turned to him.

Adam was not sure what he had expected, but this man was not it. The gardener was slightly stooped and his hands were calloused, but his weathered face was softened by a welcoming smile that made Adam realize that this man could be easily approached. His eyes were intent, taking in everything without judgment. Adam was immediately drawn to this kindly caretaker of an incredible ecosystem. "I'm ready to teach you now," said the man. "You can call me Ned."

Ned waited quietly for Adam to speak. Finally, Adam asked, "What is this place, and how did you create such an incredible ecosystem?"

Ned wiped his hands on his jeans and said, "Well, I guess I was simply living out what I believe."

"But how does that work?" asked Adam. "How do your beliefs and passions actually impact something as much as you have this beautiful ecosystem?"

"That's easy," replied Ned. "You see, when you act in ways that are true to who you are, good things can happen. My team knows that I am true to my word, and they sense that I am committed to what we are striving to create. Nothing is more powerful than that!"

One of the basic tenets of nature is integrity within each species. For instance, a tomato plant will grow tomatoes, not corn. An oak tree will grow acorns, which create more oak trees, not maples. A collie gives birth to collies, not Saint Bernards. This integrity within species is so consistent that it makes further explanation unnecessary. All species, in effect, are true to their nature and identity.

Likewise, the first key to natural leadership consists of character and integrity. Integrity is upholding consistency in our thoughts, words, and actions. One of the ways that your team will evaluate your integrity is through how well they can predict what you will do, the decisions you will make, and how you will react. There is security in knowing who a person is inside, what they value, and what they stand for in the face of adversity. Integrity and trust are the bedrocks of relationships and allow people to work in harmony with each other. Only then can people demonstrate respect and work interdependently.

A great example of integrity was reported several years ago, when a regional manager for a large grocery chain protected consumers in the face of a poison scare. Along with his usual shipment of produce, this manager had also received an anonymous letter stating that the produce had been intentionally poisoned. There was no way to know for sure if the produce was good or not. But the value of the produce was in the hundreds of thousands of dollars. He had to ask himself, should he risk keeping the produce and potentially put his clients' health at risk? Or should he throw the produce out and lose all that money?

The regional manager made the difficult but correct decision to throw out the produce. He would not squander his integrity just to make money. The message to his customers was clear: they would always come first in his eyes. Therefore, this manager has gained the loyalty of many customers who trust and rely on him for quality products. Moreover, his exemplary actions were reported in the *Grand Rapids Press* and other periodicals. The publicity generated by this manager's decision produced great benefits for the grocery chain. That's why integrity is key for natural leaders! The negative implications for themselves, their teams, and their clients if they fail to act with integrity are tremendous.

Natural leaders understand that once their team stops trusting them or stops believing that whom and what they represent is "for real," their leadership is lost. People will not follow you without knowing that you are genuine and honest with them. Team members will not believe that what you are doing is in their best interests.

Likewise, if clients suspect that you are not being honest with them, they will either leave immediately or will only remain loyal until a better offer comes along. When given a comparable choice, clients will gravitate toward honest leaders and organizations. Organizations that stand behind their promises are the ones that will rise to the top and sustain long-term growth.

Assessing yourself

Just as others are assessing their integrity, leaders will assess their own integrity in a variety of ways. The first assessments we must make are in those quiet moments when we are alone. In *Who You Are When No One's Looking*, Bill Hybels poses one of the greatest tests of our integrity. He challenges us to define our integrity by what we would do if no one were to ever find out what we have done.[2] In those moments when we are alone and are free to act at will, what choices do we make? It is a daunting task

2   Bill Hybels, *Who You Are When No One's Looking: Choosing Consistency, Resisting Compromise* (Downers Grove: InterVarsity Press, 1987).

to master our integrity and discipline ourselves to act consistently with what we know we should do.

Integrity also means owing up to your mistakes. For example, early in my career, I assisted a coworker with hiring a plant worker. When our client asked who had responded to our ad, I gave out the names, not knowing that one of the candidates was already employed by our client. To say that our client was upset and angry would be to put it mildly. I could have hidden my error and not said anything to my coworker about what had happened. But I knew the right decision was to admit my error and contact the applicant to warn him about the situation. My coworker warned me the candidate might be very angry and urged me not to contact him. I insisted on contacting this person, knowing that there would be repercussions for him at work. My integrity was on the line, and I could not fail to do what was right.

As a result, my coworkers gained even more respect for my leadership, and the candidate who was involved understood the situation and was grateful we contacted him. As an organization, we gained loyalty from the people we served by doing what was right.

Shaping your thoughts

To be leaders of integrity, we must start with our thoughts, for out of our thoughts will develop attitudes and then actions. An easy way to prove this is to talk to anyone who has been on a diet. They say they want to lose weight and plan to eat only healthy, low-calorie foods. However, as time goes by, they start thinking about all the tasty desserts they used to eat. They think about how wonderful it would be to have just a little bit of that dessert now. Pretty soon, their attitude is that they have worked hard and deserve that dessert, maybe even *need* to eat that dessert along with everyone else. All their wonderful thoughts about losing weight disappear, and they find themselves indulging their desires.

If we are to be leaders of integrity, we must guard our thoughts. This means we must guard what enters our minds from outside sources; we must choose with care the books we read, the music we listen to, and the companions we talk with on a regular basis. All of the messages we receive begin to impact our thoughts and therefore our attitudes and actions. Integrity of thought means that we will focus on positive and constructive ideas, which will enable us to act on our values.

In this manner, we can shape our attitudes through consistent, constant effort. For example, some of my clients struggle with self-confidence and worry. A helpful exercise I recommend is to make a list of the top ten things they're good at. Then I ask them to review this list every morning and every evening for a month. At the end of the month, when we talk again about their view of themselves, the difference in their attitude is amazing. Instead of constantly thinking negative thoughts about themselves, they begin thinking positive thoughts, and it changes their entire perspective. They no longer second-guess their actions, but become able to make decisions quickly. Their newfound self-confidence also spills over into their relationships with their teammates. Their peers gain respect for them and listen to their input during group discussions.

Speaking the truth

Not only must we master the integrity of our thoughts, but we must also master the integrity of our words. When we speak, our words must be consistent with what we have said on other occasions and to other people. Nothing undermines our integrity faster than when we say one thing to someone and then turn around and say something else to another person.

Some leaders want to please people and be popular with everyone. Therefore, they go out of their way to say what others wish to hear, even if it is not true. Unfortunately, their popularity is short-lived because they are not consistent and people do not trust them. Team members create their own interpretation of what these leaders "really" meant, instead of relying on what they are being told.

Other leaders want to avoid conflict. They know that the truth will be difficult for people to hear, and so they sidestep the truth in hopes of putting off the confrontation. The key when sharing difficult news is demonstrating to people that you care about the impact of the information on them. However, you must make sure that you deliver the difficult news along with how you desire to assist them with the impact of this information. People can accept that there will be difficult days ahead or difficult aspects of their work, as long as they know you care and understand the implications for them.

For example, an executive director of a medical facility was once charged with making many difficult changes in her operation. These changes would necessitate hard work for the team and a willingness to change long-standing practices. The executive director went to the team, told them the direction that needed to be adopted, listened to their concerns, and then expressed appreciation for the hard work and commitment the team was providing. The team was then willing to support the new projects and adopt new processes, since they realized their efforts were valued and appreciated. As a result, the team was able to take their operation to the next level, meeting the timelines established at the beginning of the project. Additionally, the team was excited about the changes and their new accomplishments. Morale improved, and the organization as a whole was positioned to excel as never before.

This executive director left a very small carbon footprint since she was honest about the challenges ahead. Her team responded with trust and renewed energy to see the project through. Her legacy will be felt long after this difficult period and will continue to produce positive results.

Demonstrating consistency

When leaders have mastered integrity of thought and word, the next step is to master integrity of action. Our actions always send messages to our team members and those around us. Most leaders do the best they can and trust that others will understand their intent. But in fact, this is rarely the case; even when leaders think they are being consistent with their words, they may be doubted and misinterpreted by their team if they don't explain their actions. Indeed, since consistency between our words and actions is so critical, we can never leave it to chance that people will correctly interpret our actions. This is because whenever people do not understand something, they will create an explanation for what we have done. These explanations will be predominately negative.

Therefore, as leaders it is imperative that our actions match our verbal communication. Natural leaders will work to ensure that their teams know why they are taking certain steps. Effective leaders will share not only the "what" but also the "why" of their actions. This technique will help to eliminate misconceptions and mistrust based on misinterpretation of our actions.

For example, while working with a manager in an engineering firm who expressed a desire for his team to succeed, we discovered that his team actually felt belittled and unable to please him. The manager would communicate that he believed in the team's ability to succeed, but then would micromanage the project and ultimately take back the task when things did not go well. The manager was a perfectionist and had a very different approach from others on the team, which created difficulty when training, delegating, and evaluating his team members. The team therefore assumed that the manager did not respect them or support their growth professionally. Soon, people were asking to be removed from the team. In fact, it got so bad that the organization removed all of their direct reports from them. If this rings a bell for you, then develop the self-awareness to avoid a similar fate.

Fortunately, the situation was eventually alleviated. Our consulting firm began working with this manager and demonstrating a more effective way of delegating, monitoring, and leading his team. We increased his self-awareness and ability to use diverse communication styles when working with various members of his team. Through this process he was able to regain the respect of others and returned to management status. Today, he enjoys a strong reputation and the loyalty of those who now report to him.

Your team will always watch your actions to understand more about you, your priorities, and how to succeed. Therefore leaders need to be careful with their actions to ensure that they send the proper message. Every day, you have opportunities to reinforce your values and vision. These opportunities can produce wonderful results when you choose your actions wisely.

Integrity is simple, and yet extremely difficult for leaders to maintain. Leaders feel pressured to make higher profits, add new clients, and respond to the needs of clients and staff. In the midst of pressure from the economy and from others, it is difficult to maintain your focus and resolve. However, your carbon footprint will increase without this necessary foundation of integrity.

Assess Your Natural Leadership: Integrity

1. On a scale of 1 to 5, with 5 being best, how would you rate your integrity?

2. When no one is around, are there times when you act in ways that are inconsistent with your values?

3. Are there people who know you well enough to ask the tough questions about your integrity?

4. When you have a difficult decision to make, do you delay telling others to avoid a confrontation with them?

5. If someone made a silent movie of you at work, what messages would your audience see in your actions?

Chapter 2:

Initiative

"But how and why did you decide to create this beautiful ecosystem?" asked Adam. "I can't imagine the work that has gone into creating and maintaining such a breathtaking environment."

"To be sure, it's been a lot of work," said Ned. "In fact, it takes far more work to maintain this ecosystem correctly than it would to just do things the fast, easy way. But that leads to a shallow experience that isn't fulfilling for anyone. You see, long ago I felt dissatisfied with the way things were around me. I saw sick and dying plants and animals, and I saw people misusing natural resources. I was unhappy until I realized that I could actually do something about it. So I began developing a plan to shape something very different. What you see is the result of those early efforts."

Not that long ago, we as a country were fairly naive about the challenges we were creating in the environment. We assumed everything was fine and that there would be an unlimited, everlasting supply of resources. Finally, a few leaders called our attention to the problems that we were creating in the environment. These leaders understood the dangers that would be created if our practices did not change. Therefore, they took steps to warn people everywhere about their concerns.

Naysayers made jokes about global warming theories and other environmental problems. They disparaged the leaders who raised these concerns. But these leaders had the uncomfortable and difficult job of delivering the bad news. We either had to start changing our habits or we would lose much of the natural beauty and resources we already enjoyed.

However, today, due in large part to those early warnings, further studies have been conducted that show their concerns were well-founded. We see glaciers melting and habitats changing due to the small changes in the earth's temperature. Those small changes in temperature are producing large results that will have an untold impact on our future.

Likewise, business leaders realize that small things that go unchecked will have a tremendous impact on their cultures and organizations. It's not only the glaring issues of terrorist attacks or shaky economies that cripple organizations. More often, it is the small changes that we allow to creep in and pollute our culture that undermine our future.

Therefore, natural leaders are attuned to watching for those "small" changes and responding quickly. While others ignore the changes and suggest that they do not matter, natural leaders take initiative to guard against negative change. They understand that the nature of these problems is to grow and spread throughout organizations. It is imperative that leaders stay on guard and watch for changes that can send their team down a destructive path.

The principle of actively guarding your organization leads us to the second key of natural leadership, which is initiative. Initiative, by definition, is impacting your environment instead of responding to the circumstances around you. Leaders must not hesitate when action is needed. Without the willingness and ability to initiate, leaders will not be able to shape the future, gain momentum, or ensure success for their team.

Righting a wrong

One of the ways in which leaders must display initiative is in working to right a wrong or correct a mistake. Where others may notice the problem and just walk by, leaders refuse to look the other way, but rather act to correct the situation. Natural leaders show initiative, not only by bringing the problem to light, but also by working toward a solution.

Many people enjoy pointing out and calling attention to problems. They almost seem to take pleasure in telling us about all the ills in our world. However, this is not leadership. Complaining about a problem is just negativity, no matter how creatively you phrase your comments. True leadership lies in resolving issues quickly and effectively so that everyone will benefit from your work.

You need only to look at some of the great leaders of our day to see poignant examples of this principle. Martin Luther King Jr. saw the injustice of racism and took steps to correct it long before the idea of equal rights gained widespread acceptance. He stepped out and called people to take action, even though doing so created controversy and endangered his personal safety. However, his principles and values demanded that he act rather than wait for someone else to do the hard work. In part due to his actions, we now benefit from a much more open and accepting country. There is much more work to be done to bring about true equality, but each generation, each organization, and each family needs leaders like Martin Luther King Jr. who are willing to initiate and lead the way for others.

Creating momentum

Natural leaders also understand the need to initiate projects that will score small wins for the team. Such small successes allow the team to move forward and lead to larger victories down the road. Growth and momentum will not come from simply wishing that good things will happen. Growth comes from creating new direction and initiating specific actions that will lead the team forward.

For example, in the early 1980s, Grand Rapids, Michigan, had a downtown area that was in danger of becoming fairly lifeless and unattractive to visitors. However, in 1981, Amway Corporation saw an opportunity to impact the greater Grand Rapids community for the better. They purchased the Pantlind Hotel (now called the Amway Grand Plaza Hotel) and began an extensive renovation and expansion of the facility. Today, it is a beautiful, four-star hotel that has hosted US presidents and many other dignitaries. That spark they created in 1981 has translated into a much more vibrant downtown area for Grand Rapids. Impressive hotels, a convention center that hosts large, diverse groups, an arena for sports and entertainment, new businesses, museums, medical institutions, and restaurants have all been added since those early efforts. Now, when visitors come to downtown Grand Rapids, they experience vitality and a diverse, cultural city. The city has reaped the economic benefits of all this activity and has developed a much more positive reputation in the region.

All of this transformation is exciting, but it began with one leader of an organization who took the initiative. He could have waited until someone else took the first step toward revitalization. Instead, he acted on something he knew was imperative for the area and good for his company. As a result, his leadership has grown, as has the company's reputation.

Balancing efforts

Imbalance in the environment creates dangerous conditions, since plants or wildlife that become too prevalent endanger other species. An environmental imbalance also creates a drain on certain resources, thus making it difficult for even the dominant plant or animal to survive. Only through a balanced environment can there be a healthy, thriving, and sustainable ecosystem.

Likewise, when our teams or organizations are internally imbalanced, the results will be crippling. Imbalances often arise when we spend too much time or money in one area, while neglecting another. Imagine the disastrous results of spending almost all your resources on research and development and very little on marketing. You may have well-designed, effective products, but if no one knows about them, you will go out of business.

In a similar fashion, if you hire a lot of people in sales but very few in support services, you'll face disaster. You may get a lot of sales orders, but you will lose customers quickly, since they will not receive the level of service promised. Your sales team will have to work harder to acquire additional sales as your reputation for customer service becomes questionable.

As another example, many organizations prioritize obtaining new clients. To be sure, every organization needs to continually gain new clients, but if you take your current clients for granted, you will ultimately lose momentum. Your current clients will begin to look for someone else who will take care of their needs rather than ignoring them. Your sales efforts will not have created momentum, but rather a revolving door that will frustrate the entire team.

Natural leaders understand the need to initiate corrections in order to maintain balance. This means that leaders must be aware of their own preferences and guard against overindulging themselves. We all have areas that we love to work on within our organization. It may be that we are born salespeople, or strategists, or financial analysts. We could easily spend our entire day absorbed in one aspect of the business without ever thinking about the rest of the organization. This tendency, if not held in check, will lead to imbalance and chaos.

For example, I once knew a business owner who loved to work on processes and systems. He was in charge of a manufacturing company, and he spent countless hours perfecting the internal processes of the business. However, he spent very little time on obtaining sales. When asked about his sales efforts, he would respond that he knew he should spend more time on that area, but didn't have enough time to do so. Therefore, weeks would pass before he would pick up the phone to make a sales call. Profits continued to drop, and the company was in danger of closing due to lack of sales. This leader's lack of balance in his time and attention almost drove this company into bankruptcy.

Natural leaders will right an imbalance and ensure that there is an infusion of resources, new ideas, clients, and staff to maintain that balance. They anticipate organizational needs and seek out the critical resources to meet those needs. They evaluate the organization for weak areas and strive to strengthen those areas to promote further growth.

Preventing problems

We have spent much of this chapter discussing ways in which leaders step forward to address existing issues. While this is a very important characteristic, natural leaders also proactively look ahead to anticipate and prevent potential problems. While others around them are busy reacting to the problems, natural leaders plan, strategize, and create momentum. Their goal is to stay ahead of trends and changes in the marketplace.

Being proactive requires leaders to be disciplined with their time, attention, and resources. They must commit sufficient time to thinking about the big picture, the future, trends, and opportunities. Planning becomes a regular part of their schedule and a skill they hone. Natural leaders resist the urge to constantly be in motion, knowing that by being proactive, they will outpace the chaotic efforts of their competitors.

Julie Lough, president of Micro Visions, is an excellent example of this principle. Micro Visions is an IT firm that provides consulting services. Lough has maintained excellence in her organization through planning and anticipating client needs. For example, Lough recently sensed that prospective clients were frustrated because their IT firms couldn't give them cost estimates and charged unpredictably. So Lough and her team have created a service package to manage their clients' IT needs for a set monthly fee. Her clients love it because the service prevents rather than reacts to problems, can be easily budgeted, and includes strategic IT planning and guidance.

Without this kind of forethought, companies often find themselves in trouble. A classic example occurs in many companies when they realize sales are down. They react by spending all their time and energy marketing their products or services. Sales come in, so then they stop selling and spend all their time servicing the sales they've received. However, sales and profits then drop, so they return to a frenzy of marketing and sales. This roller-coaster process is costly and counterproductive to long-term, sustainable growth.

Natural leaders fight this tendency by proactively managing their time and looking ahead to anticipate the needs of their organization and clients. Being proactive minimizes their need to put out fires and instead keeps them focused on the imperatives that will allow them to thrive even in a tough economy and achieve long-term success. Natural leaders are agile in responding to change, resulting in maximum growth and profitability.

Assess Your Natural Leadership: Initiative

1. On a scale of 1 to 5, with 1 being a long time and 5 being immediate, how long does it typically take you to correct a wrong?

2. How have you initiated projects that score wins for your team?

3. How are you avoiding the temptation to indulge in "pet" projects while ignoring other critical areas of growth?

4. How much time on average are you investing in long-term planning?

Chapter 3:

Courage

Adam was impressed with Ned's accomplishments over the years. It was awe-inspiring to look around and see the beauty within the ecosystem. "How did you keep all this going? I would have been overwhelmed by the sheer size of the task," he said.

Ned paused for a moment, reflecting back on the years he had spent nurturing the ecosystem. "You're right about this being overwhelming at times. People come here and see the beauty, but they don't realize the hard work that has gone into continuing the growth and maintaining something as large as this. There have been times when it would have been easier to give up and just let someone else take over.

"But as a leader, I knew that the team was counting on me not to quit. So I drew deep from within to keep going. As a result, my team members have stayed committed and true to our mission, and we've accomplished so much together. You see, without courage, not much of true importance or value is accomplished."

Every species faces daily challenges and obstacles. Some face natural predators, while others face prey that's difficult to catch. However, animals face these obstacles because it is a must for survival. They instinctively act with "courage" and grow into these new experiences and challenges. At times, they face overwhelming odds—such as when salmon must swim upstream—but they do whatever is necessary to ensure the continuation of their species.

Humans, on the other hand, must *decide* to act with courage in the face of obstacles; for most of us, it doesn't come naturally. For example, when a fire erupts within a wildlife area, it is only through courage that firefighters respond. They understand the dangers but refuse to stay where it is safe. Instead, they move in toward the fire and work to protect the wildlife and ecosystems at risk. They take calculated risks to achieve their goals, knowing that time is of the essence.

In a similar fashion, courage is the third key of corporate leadership. For without courage, we would not take the risk of acting first. We would wait for others in order to avoid mistakes. Age-old excuses, such as "We've never done it this way before," are simply another way of saying that we are afraid of failing. It takes courage to act and to lead.

Most of us receive false impressions of what constitutes "courage" from our surrounding culture. For example, most action-movie heroes laugh in the face of danger and are willing to engage in Superman-type activities. They seem fearless even when the odds are against them. However, courage is not about being fearless. Courage is rather the ability to move forward and act even when we are afraid.

For example, every entrepreneur knows what it is to be afraid, whether they have been in business for two minutes, two weeks, or two months. The challenges before them are great. Those challenges can include difficult economic conditions, tough competition, changes in operating costs, and more. In fact, roughly 50 percent of all businesses fail in the first year. However, successful leaders face their fears and move forward, knowing that the rewards outweigh the difficulties.

Facing adversity

Natural leaders exhibit courage and strength in the face of adversity. They know there will be costs but strive to achieve something better and more meaningful for others. They step into the gap and point out the way for others. Their courage and steadfastness provides strength for those who follow.

Franklin D. Roosevelt was a great example when he spoke to the United States and the world during World War II. His statement, "We have nothing to fear but fear itself," demonstrated courage when others were paralyzed by fear. As a result, others responded, and the Alliance was victorious in the face of daunting obstacles.

Likewise, in organizations, natural leaders know the importance of standing in the gap during times of trouble. It is easy to be a leader when things are going well for an organization. The real test of strong leaders is when things are going poorly. Do they run and hide? Or do they step forward with conviction, ready to pave the way for the team? Being a leader means that we must be willing to take difficult steps, make difficult decisions, and act decisively even when success is not assured.

As I meet with business owners and decision makers, I am continually impressed with their courage. Some business owners face economic hardship, some have lost key employees, and some are facing difficult transitions within their markets and industries. However, those who succeed see these difficulties as doors to new opportunities. They display courage in finding ways through the problems, instead of being crushed by them.

For example, I once knew an area business owner who received the difficult news that an overseas operation had been shut down by the host country's government, through no fault of his company. The company assets, which were considerable, had been taken by the government, and all that was left were the members of his team. Everyone who heard the news was in shock and could not think of how this business leader could ever recover.

Instead of shutting his doors and admitting defeat, this leader decided that, since his team was depending on him for their livelihood, he was going to find a way through this terrible problem. So he looked at the natural resources of the region and the hot industries that were developing and discovered another product they could create. He directed his team to begin investigating those possibilities, and was able to keep his team together while he looked for a new long-term direction for his business. As a result, his business resumed, the team stayed together, and his company remained profitable.

These actions were truly very courageous on his part, since there was no guarantee that the same government that closed down his other operation would not do the same with this one. He also could not be sure his team would agree to move in a whole new direction, especially since it entailed entering an industry in which he had no prior experience. But he, like many natural leaders, had the courage to take those steps even in the midst of adversity. By refusing to give in and become victims of circumstance, he and other natural leaders instead found ways to become stronger and better because of those challenges.

Taking responsibility

Natural leaders have not only the courage to face adversity but also the courage to admit errors. When mistakes are made, they do not hide behind corporate policy and loopholes. They step up to the plate, admit that they made a mistake, and offer to correct that error. Their customers know that they will stand behind their products and services and deliver exactly what they promised.

This can be difficult, especially when you realize that correcting an error could cost you money or harm your reputation. It's tempting to cover up the error, or to blame someone else in the organization. Leaders can never give in to these temptations, or they will face serious repercussions. Team members will lose respect for them, clients will realize that the company is growing at their expense, and their companies will begin to falter.

The president of Advance Caster and Wheel, Eric Butler, provides a good example of this type of courage. His company sells casters and wheels to many different industries across the country. They have a strong quality-control program and pride themselves on delivering just what the customer needs on time. In one instance, though, they delivered casters that were not up to a client's specifications. When their customer called to complain about the problem, Eric Butler asked to go out and investigate the problem. After a careful review of the problem, he told the client that Advance Caster had erred and they wanted to correct the problem at no cost to the client. The problem was resolved, and to this day that client is still loyal because of Butler's courage in doing what was right.

Butler then went a step further and reviewed internal processes to evaluate what went wrong. He quickly located the issue, corrected it, and ensured that the problem would not reoccur. Today they are rated an A+ preferred vendor by an international company based on their quality and ability to deliver results. Butler's courage to admit their mistake and to take responsibility turned what could have been a damaging situation into a very positive outcome.

Staying the course

Not only do natural leaders have the courage to face adversity and to admit and correct errors, but they also have the courage to stay the course.

In a world where we want everything *now*, leaders often face the temptation of thinking only in the short term. Their corporate boards are asking them for results now, not later. It is as if they expect leaders to wave a magic wand, and the results will materialize before their eyes. However, the most important things take time and nurturing to develop.

The desire for approval, the focus on looking good for constituents, and the drive to achieve can all lead us to focus on the short term even when we know there will be consequences down the road. These pressures are significant and can falsely guide leaders in the wrong direction.

Natural leaders know that by staying the course, even when they cannot see the results, they can accomplish great things. They have the courage to persevere when others falter and give up. These leaders know that persevering will ensure success and multiply results.

Many people begin new ventures, only to wonder why they are not seeing immediate results. They give up just when good things are about to happen. Their courage wanes, and they decide to take an easier path. No one said that success or leadership were easy. If that were true, all of us would be successful in our endeavors.

However, successful endeavors are like seeds we plant in the ground. As much as we want flowers to appear as soon as the seeds are planted, we all know it would be unrealistic to expect that to really happen. We have to nurture those seeds and create the right conditions for flowers to bloom.

Every process has to unfold and develop over the course of time. As much as we want to shorten that time, we must allow the process to continue for good things to materialize. Leaders who have the courage to stay the course in anticipation of future results will reap rich rewards.

A beautiful example of this principle is the Frederick Meijer Gardens and Sculpture Park in Grand Rapids, Michigan. The conservatory was started in 1995. Initially, it lacked the richness and diversity of more mature gardens.

Now, some thirteen years later, the Frederick Meijer Gardens and Sculpture Park has become a conservatory with depth, richness, beauty, and harmony. It has taken time and tremendous investment to bring out that beauty. The formula for creating the gardens is simple in theory and yet takes a lifelong passion to truly implement. Today there are over ten different gardens that are unique, beautiful, and awe-inspiring. The gardens, landscaping, and sculptures all merge to create breathtaking vistas.

Likewise, natural leaders live out their courage day by day, month by month, and year by year. We see leaders' courage as they take risks to reinvest themselves and resources in their endeavors. We see courage displayed as leaders step out into new markets, new projects, and new ways of looking at the world. Courage is not required solely for the bigger-than-life moments, but also for the everyday existence in which our hopes meet reality.

Assess Your Natural Leadership: Courage

1. In what specific ways are you leading your team through the tough times?

2. When an error comes to light, do you quickly own the problem or look for someone to blame?

3. Do you persevere through obstacles to reach goals or quickly give up when a challenge arises?

4. Do you take needed risks to propel your company forward?

Chapter 4:

Learning and Self-renewal

Adam was awestruck by the wisdom and insights Ned shared with him. "How do you know so much? You seem so wise!"

Ned shrugged. "As much as I've learned over the years, there is still so much I do not know and want to learn. You see that plant over there?" Ned pointed to a plant over on the edge of a clearing.

Adam nodded as he focused on the plant Ned had indicated.

"That plant looks healthy and strong, but it's not growing. I'm not sure what is wrong with it. Even slow-growing plants would have grown more than this one has. So I'm doing research and trying to learn more about the needs of that particular plant," said Ned.

"You must really care to continue learning after all this time," said Adam. "How do you find time for it all? You must be exhausted!"

"Well, some days can be tiring, but I make sure I get enough rest, and I even take one day a month just to enjoy myself and participate in some other hobbies. Most people aren't aware of this, but I love to cook. I'm actually trying out some new vegetarian recipes right now. You'll have to stay for lunch and try some of my experiments," said Ned.

In nature, there is a cycle, or natural sequence, to everything. In seasonal climates, trees lose their leaves in the fall, are dormant in the winter, and re-emerge with new growth through the spring and summer. While trees cease growing in the winter, they're storing critical nutrients to fuel that next season of growth. We see this same principle in insects. Caterpillars will spin a cocoon and spend weeks or even months transforming and growing before finally emerging as butterflies. They require a period of rest before they have the capacity to grow. There is an ebb and flow to everything in nature.

In a similar fashion, leaders must take time to renew or refuel themselves between busy periods. This fourth key of leadership, self-renewal, underscores the importance of rest, reflection, self-evaluation, and lifelong learning. Engaging in these activities will bolster your wisdom, creativity, and leadership ability. Just as we need to plan and take initiative, we must also take the time for self-renewal.

Continuing education

Self-renewal should be continuous throughout our lives. This principle is true whether things are going poorly or extremely well. Leaders are constantly giving a lot of energy to those around them, and this level of activity will tend to drain their energy and resilience. If leaders ignore the signals of fatigue long enough, they eventually burn out.

Resting

Many leaders incorrectly assume that they can ignore their need for rest and keep going, even when they are low on energy. They give in to the tendency to keep working long after they lose the ability to be productive. When leaders do so, their work will be of poor quality and they will take longer to accomplish their tasks.

Leaders also fail to make time for rest because they believe being extremely busy all the time increases their value to their organizations. Leaders fill their days from beginning to end with meetings and then struggle to accomplish everything else after-hours. They are drained mentally and emotionally and have little energy left over for any creative thought. This depletion of their resilience will actually decrease their value and effectiveness.

I knew one leader who worked such long days that he had almost no balance in his life. He would take his cell phone with him on vacation and would check his messages frequently throughout the day, so he was never fully able to relax. In fact, when he returned from vacation, he reflected that he was more exhausted than when he'd left, because emotionally and mentally he'd never left work. In turn, his performance declined, and he was ultimately asked to leave the organization. While he had once been a key leader, he now had become someone who could no longer contribute and be productive.

The importance of making self-renewal a priority is clear. Self-renewal includes taking time for relaxation, stimulating conversation, education, and reflection on current trends. Creativity is impossible without rest, exercise, and exposure to new ideas. You won't have the ability to grasp new concepts and think outside the box unless you renew your mind, body, and emotions.

As another example, I knew of a national speaker who was constantly on the go and worked incredible hours. She was well-known and accepted continuous requests to speak at conferences across the country. She would often get off one plane and jump on another to go to the next conference. While she was passionate about sharing her expertise with audiences, she was draining herself in every way. One day in an airport, she collapsed from exhaustion. She was rushed to a hospital and underwent treatment for a week. Her recuperation took another six weeks, after which she could begin working on a part-time basis. A total of seven weeks gone, just like that!

Most leaders do not experience something as dramatic as this speaker did. However, many find that they arrive in the morning physically and mentally tired. They resort to caffeine to jump-start their days. This strategy will work in the short term, but not in the long term. Eventually, our bodies will begin to break down and succumb to ailments. The price tag at that point is so significant health-wise that many people never fully recover from it.

Self-evaluating

Just as leaders must engage in periods of rest, they must also engage in self-reflection on a regular basis. As leaders, we must continuously ask ourselves how we should change and do things differently in order to thrive. It is not simply a matter of how good we are today, or what we know now. The answers we possess today will not meet the challenges and threats of tomorrow.

Natural leaders often ask, "What changes can I make to my leadership style, and what new things do I need to learn in order to have the greatest impact?" In order to answer these questions, they must view themselves accurately, which is often a difficult task. However, failure to see themselves accurately can cripple leaders' efforts to lead the organization forward.

For example, I knew a CEO of a large company who was frustrated because his managers did not seem to make independent decisions. He felt they were not creative or willing to take risks when faced with new situations. Their profits and growth had hit a plateau for a number of years, and his frustration grew. He felt that he had empowered his team to make decisions, but instead they were reluctant to take action.

However, when we began talking with some of the key people in the company, they began to describe the CEO as someone who micromanaged their work. In fact, one of the examples they shared shed new light on the situation. A committee had looked into identifying a new vendor for their coffee and related supplies. While the CEO was away on vacation, they had selected a vendor and had the new coffee delivered. Upon returning from his vacation, the CEO discovered that a new vendor had been selected, tasted the coffee, and promptly told them to get rid of the new vendor. He wanted the old vendor and coffee returned immediately. In other words, he undermined their independent decision and micromanaged.

His inability to view himself accurately was very costly. The organization's growth was stymied since he had stopped growing and was not even aware of the issues in his leadership style. His attention was focused on those around him, instead of on assessing his behavior and strengths.

Therefore, leaders need to use a variety of tools to understand the impact of their own attitudes and actions. Examples of such tools can include conducting a 360-degree evaluation,[3] soliciting feedback from coworkers and peers who will be honest with us, reading leadership books, and using leadership profiles such as DISC.[4] These self-evaluation tools can greatly benefit us.

One such benefit is that we learn to prioritize critical areas of our professional development. There are many areas we could target in our

---

3   360 Degree Evaluations ask for feedback from those around the leader. Feedback can come from direct reports, peers, supervisors, clients, or any other groups the leader interacts with.

4   DISC is a behavioral profile system that allows insight into our natural tendencies and preferences. It focuses on work-related behavior and was created and sold by Inscape Publishing.

professional development, but identifying the most impactful areas takes thought and evaluation. Obtaining objective feedback and insight is imperative to this process.

Second, self-evaluation also helps us work on a variety of important areas, not just our favorite ones. Some of us enjoy learning about a particular aspect of our work. We thrive on researching the latest information related to that area. However, if we repeatedly focus only on one area of development, we will neglect other crucial areas of our development. Therefore, using assessment tools will ensure that we have a well-rounded development plan. It's important to keep in mind that we all have weak areas, since being strong in one area often requires that we are weak in another. For example, if you are very systematic and organized, you may not be as strong at creative activity, since the two use very different skill sets. It is part of the human makeup to possess both strengths and weaknesses.

The third benefit leaders receive from self-evaluation is an accurate view of themselves. Some individuals are overly critical of their faults and neglect their strengths. Likewise, if leaders tend to be overly positive about their strengths, self-assessment can reveal those areas in need of improvement. These insights will keep leaders from being overly confident, which could otherwise hinder professional growth.

Evolving

Natural leaders are driven by excellence. They set high standards for themselves and strive to learn more so as to advance their organizations. Successful leaders are avid readers, attend conferences and workshops, spend time meeting with counterparts, and in some cases, with their competitors. They are always scanning the horizon for new ideas, new trends, and new information that will guide them in meeting future needs.

Since natural leaders are listening, looking, and staying attuned to the environment around them, they are prepared to quickly adapt to needed changes. They are less likely to feel overwhelmed or insecure when new challenges arise, and will often be able to draw on their knowledge and insights.

One such leader is John Karle, executive vice-president for Crosby & Henry, which provides personal and commercial insurance. Karle is constantly seeking out new opportunities for growth and welcomes feedback on his performance. He receives coaching, reads books, attends workshops, and seeks out other learning opportunities to continue sharpening his skills.

Karle has even coined a word that describes this process perfectly. He states that you have to be "helpable" if you want to succeed. Helpable means that we stay open for others to assist us in our development and in reaching our goals. Leaders who are helpable will continue to look for feedback from those around them. "Helpable" describes this process of continually striving to improve and grow our skills.

One of the best ways to achieve professional development is to have an annual plan which identifies the areas you wish to develop, the strategies and tools for doing so, and timelines for each step. As with any goal, forming a strategy is critical for reaching your intended outcomes. For example, if you decided through self-examination that you needed to improve your ability to resolve conflict, that would be a good place to begin. However, unless you also develop a strategy for doing so, your chances of success are very limited.

When creating a professional development plan, leaders also need to incorporate a wide variety of tools. Today, many nontraditional tools for professional development are available. For instance, instead of traveling to conferences, you could choose to complete online classes or webinars. These allow you to learn while eliminating the expense of traveling.

Another tool many natural leaders are turning to is coaching. Professional coaching can condense and speed up the learning curve. Since the coach has already mastered the area in which you need to grow and can quickly customize the concepts and information to relate to your situation, you can quickly gain a maximum impact through coaching. A good coach also encourages you to continue learning and will ensure that you are implementing your growth strategies.

As an example, we once coached the rising star of a large, international company. She was promoted to a mid-level management position with only two years of supervisory experience. She became the leader of twelve other people, many of whom had been her peers prior to this promotion. She was charged not only with leading the team in their office but also with coordinating and creating systems between offices.

This young manager brought us in to provide coaching and act as a guide as she began assessing the needs of the department. We assisted her in redefining her role, assessing the strengths of team members, and realigning the team with new priorities. This proved difficult, since the former manager had had few expectations and had allowed team members to work based on their personal preferences. Little time had been spent creating goals or establishing expectations. Fortunately, as a result of our work together, she was able to gain confidence in her leadership ability, provide clear direction to her team members, and receive recognition for her leadership abilities within the corporation.

Whatever tool they use, leaders can never leave their development to chance. They must guard and prioritize their development within their calendar. It is simply too crucial to overlook, not only for the success of leaders, but also for the success of the organization. We can never be too busy or too proud to continue our lifelong learning.

Assess Your Natural Leadership: Learning and Self-Renewal

1. When you arrive at work in the morning, do you typically feel energized or struggle to get going?

2. Do you spend regular time relaxing and getting refreshed?

3. Do you have an annual growth plan for yourself?

4. How are you obtaining objective feedback and evaluating your leadership style?

5. Do you have a mentor, coach, or advisors who provide insights into your professional development?

Part II:

Mastery of Purpose

Chapter 5:

Vision

Ned led Adam through the garden as they talked. Every turn they took seemed to lead to a new, breathtaking view. "How did you get involved in this work?" asked Adam.

"Well, I noticed that the ecosystem where I lived was in pretty bad shape. It was neglected and lacked many of the nutrients needed to be healthy and vibrant. As I reflected on this sad state of affairs, I started thinking about how different it could be. How wonderful it would be if someone provided the necessary resources and shaped it into the wonderful ecosystem it had the potential to be. Gradually a vision of what you see today emerged, and I just knew that it was what I wanted to accomplish," Ned replied. "Then, as others asked about my work, and I shared the vision of what I was trying to create, many of them were willing to donate materials or volunteer their time. It has been so exciting to see others share my passion for nature and to create something unique."

In nature, when animals are blinded, their lives are immediately put in great danger. Without vision, most animals are at total risk and either die or must depend on the aid of others to survive.

In a similar fashion, if organizations do not have a clear vision of their purpose, then their well-being and sustainability are compromised. They will lack focus and direction, become susceptible to every shift in the market, and find it difficult to overcome obstacles. These factors in turn will lead to fractured and disjointed organizations that will struggle for survival.

A number of years ago, I met the owners of an athletic supplies company. The owners had been friends for a number of years and enjoyed many of the same interests. One evening, they struck up a conversation about their shared dream of founding a business that would incorporate their love of sports. They soon launched such a business.

The early days were exciting; they gained several clients, and they felt that success would soon be theirs. However, a fundamental problem soon began to plague their business. The two owners had very different philosophies, values, and visions for the company. One of the owners wanted to focus only on making money, so he decided to limit their product line to reduce inventory expenses, which in turn put the interests of their clients second to profits. This partner was determined to be profitable even if it meant cutting corners. The other owner was interested in growing, but felt it was ethically important to continue their innovation and customer focus. He prioritized doing what was right for the customer, even if, in the short-term, it meant lower profits.

Over the course of the first few years, their disagreements grew and became obvious even to those outside the company. Finally, their differences became so great that they dissolved the company and went their separate ways. Without a common vision, the company could not withstand the challenges it faced. What could have become a very successful venture ended with very little benefit to those involved.

Shaping the future

It has been said that "without a vision, the people perish."[5] Therefore, leaders must create a vision that will clearly define and shape their future. Your vision must be compelling in nature and communicate the impact your organization wants to achieve. A clearly stated vision provides a focus and common purpose for people to work toward. It encourages people to participate in your organization's work and causes clients and vendors to recognize that there is something special in what you are creating and doing. For example, if you are a software company, then your vision can't simply be to "make software." For an organization to be great, it has to impact something important in the lives of its customers.

Vision lifts your eyes from mundane, daily tasks and instead focuses your attention on important, achievable goals. It creates energy and

5   Proverbs 29:18 (New International Version).

enthusiasm in the work your team is engaged in. It is what gets you up early in the morning and causes you to work with renewed energy.

Therefore, when a vision is important enough, people will make sacrifices in order to achieve it. Many organizations are plagued by lethargy, not because people are lazy or ignorant, but because the organizations have often failed to create a vision that anyone cares about. A good exercise is to ask yourself, "If someone read our mission statement to me, how enthused would I be to see it fulfilled?" If you are not excited about the vision and purpose you engage in daily, then the people you lead will not be either.

Most vision statements are written in vague language that conveys little meaning or passion. A good example of this is the following mission statement, obtained from a corporation's website: "Be the global leader in customer value." This statement is so broad and ambiguous that it fails to attract the people necessary to fulfill it. Likewise, let's look at another company's mission statement: "XYZ will be recognized as a great customer solutions company." This statement was created by a major corporation, but would it compel you to take action? While both vision statements project a worthwhile goal, that of being customer-driven and service-oriented, they are not enough to move people and draw them to these companies.

Natural leaders know that a vision must not only be compelling and important but also far-reaching enough to involve others. A vision that is too small or which can be accomplished solely by leaders will not spark energy and passion from others. It will remain a personal goal that will have little impact on the community in which leaders work.

A vision that is compelling requires multiple talents, energies, and strengths to accomplish. It must bring together the best people in your industry to reach your intended target. When a vision is this large, its fulfillment will demand commitment, perseverance in the face of obstacles, and passion. A vision should give people a reason to want to use their talents and abilities in *your* organization instead of in another. Therefore, you must give them a vision statement that justifies their investment of time and talent. Can you imagine a vision that's so big it would take your breath away to accomplish it? Something so grand that if you achieved it, the world would sit up and take notice of your accomplishment?

An excellent example of a powerful vision is Microsoft's mission statement. They aspire to create "experiences that combine the magic of software with the power of Internet services across a world of devices." Notice the powerful wording used here. "Creating experiences," "magic of software," "power of Internet services," and "world of devices." These phrases are both engaging and awe-inspiring. Accomplishing something like this would require a multitude of people and the utmost creativity and would have great implications for clients.

A vision creates sustainability in an organization, since it will not change often. Your vision is far-reaching and impacts the future for the long term. By nature, it is the guide through good times and hard times, through changes in personnel and clients. It becomes the anchor that keeps your organization on track and directs your efforts toward a bright future.

However, while a vision does not change often, it *is* renewable. For instance, after some time has passed and your markets and staff have evolved, it will be important to consider refining your vision. New elements of the vision may be added as you deepen your efforts to accomplish it.

Some organizations start out with a very broad, vague vision statement. As time goes on, they recognize that, while the essence of the statement is still true, their sense of what they are trying to achieve has crystallized, and they are able to express it with greater clarity. This reshaping of a vision statement keeps the vision alive and meaningful far into the future.

Going back to our example of Microsoft, it is key to note that their vision statement has deepened and grown throughout their history as a company. When they first started, their vision was reportedly "A computer on every desk and in every home." This is certainly a goal that would have been difficult to imagine when they started. However, over time that goal has been largely realized countrywide; accordingly, they saw the need to deepen and broaden their vision. Thus, they have since refined the statement to its present version.

By deepening and refreshing your vision, you allow your organization to be current and vital to yourself and the world around you. You can stay true to the essence of the vision while still incorporating current conditions and new developments. This process will also continue to engage your team and clients in a partnership that goes beyond personal gains.

Instilling purpose

Once leaders have developed their visions, they must communicate them to stockholders, clients, employees, vendors, and others in the community. Simply writing a vision statement and posting it on the wall is not sufficient. To have meaning, a vision has to come alive and be reinforced on a regular basis.

One way that leaders spread vision is through the passion they exhibit. When leaders are passionate about something, they exude enthusiasm, excitement, energy, and determination. Because they are working on something they believe in, they are willing to commit themselves to the effort needed to press forward, and that commitment is contagious.

When people are passionate, they work hard but do not feel that their labor is unpleasant. For example, if you observe people who are passionate about skiing, you will see them spending hours perfecting their technique, but to them it is a pleasure to do so. They won't gripe about having to spend time on the slopes working on their form. Instead, they will eagerly anticipate getting back out there again.

In a similar fashion, leaders who are passionate about their visions will not spend time complaining about their workloads and the challenges facing them. Why? Because natural leaders know that what they are working for is important and compelling, and they have a passion they want to share with others. Thinking negatively about all the work involved is like pouring water on the fire of vision. Instead, leaders choose to ignite that same fire of passion in others through their communication.

Communicating vision is a lot like adding fertilizer to your plants. Plants don't grow overnight, just as people don't instantly respond to your vision. It takes repetition and nurturing for visions—like plants—to bloom. A leader's regular communication of a vision is what will allow it to take root and bloom.

Leaders must nourish and grow their visions and revisit them on a regular basis. Natural leaders weave their visions into every conversation. They recognize every communication as an opportunity to reinforce and promote their visions. This repetition does not mean they are quoting their visions verbatim, but rather referencing the principles and values embedded in their visions.

Larry Yachcik, president of Porter Hills Retirement Communities & Services, is a great example of this principle. He weaves in his themes of where the company is headed, why they are doing what they are doing, and their strategy for accomplishing that vision into each of his meetings and conversations. His words evidence his passion to see Porter Hills excel and achieve great things. Yachcik always has a smile on his face, determination in his step, and a belief that obstacles can be overcome. He demonstrates a positive energy, which is focused on the vision that he and others have created for Porter Hills.

Leaders must not only talk about their visions but also model their commitment to them through personal actions. Natural leaders consistently exhibit the attributes and actions needed to embody their visions. In doing so, they bring their visions to life and impact those around them.

One way in which leaders model their visions is in their attention to certain aspects of their own projects. In their own work, what do they highlight and evaluate? If the customer is truly central to their visions and priorities, they will ask about customers and work to ensure that they are well cared for. They will work to make the customer say, "Wow!"

If their visions involve creativity and innovation, they will spend time brainstorming ways for others to engage in the development of concepts and products. They will seek new tools and resources devoted to the design of products that do not exist in the market today. In so doing, their teams will see their passion, commitment, and energy to bring their visions to fruition, and will be inspired to match their enthusiasm.

Taking action and making decisions

In addition to providing focus for the future, a vision can serve a variety of purposes in a company. For example, your vision can serve to differentiate you from your current competition. If you own a printing company, there are many others who also print material. Or if you cut hair, there are likely many other stylists in your area. What separates you from your competition? You may say that you do it better than the others, and in some cases, that may be true. But what really separates you from your competition is your vision. The "why" of what you do is more important than the "how." Your vision will impact the quality and delivery of your goods or services; it will significantly impact the image you present to prospective clients. Your vision is very personal and uniquely you, almost like a fingerprint.

Your competition can mimic the words in your mission statement, but they cannot copy the results of how you live out your vision. For that is truly personal and unique to you and your organization. It is what distinguishes the average from the great.

As a personal example, I've long been a fan of a certain coffeehouse in Kentwood, Michigan, where I often meet with clients. This coffeehouse has attracted a loyal following of customers because the staff members all have terrific attitudes and because they always go beyond the basics in serving customers. For example, whenever I order a Diet Coke, they take it a step further and ask if they can provide a separate glass with ice for my drink. Now, this may seem like a small thing—and in essence it is—but the fact that they noticed a way to be helpful and followed through on it is huge. In providing the "small" things, they are communicating that the customer is all-important.

Your actions will always speak louder than your words. Your clients will always know what is important, and what your vision for the company is. They'll know whether you're following the words of your vision statement based on how they are treated and their experience with your product or service.

Another area in which your vision can provide clarity and direction is in decision making. Leaders must integrate vision into every decision, every meeting, and every project. Every decision should reflect your vision, whether it concerns finances, facility considerations, or product refinement.

For example, I know of a nonprofit whose decisions, while well intended, ultimately undermined their vision. They served the needs of the poor and were initially located in the inner city. They were right on a bus line, so it was easy for people to get to their facility. However, after a number of years at this location, several members of their board felt that the company needed a face-lift and a better facility to represent their organization. They were concerned that donors might not feel comfortable in their current location.

So they began a search for new property, and ultimately decided to relocate several miles away. This relocation afforded them more space and nicer décor. However, it meant that they were no longer on the bus line. The clients they served were not able to reach them easily without public transportation, reducing their service volume and thus impacting their ability to receive additional grants.

Natural leaders would have never approved of that decision. They would have looked at the company's mission to serve the poor and would have understood the implications of moving to that particular location. They would have chosen instead to renovate the current space or find a better facility that was still on the bus line. Leaders lose credibility with their teams when the decisions they make do not support their visions.

Managing resources

In caring for ecosystems, the National Park Service has learned to appreciate the benefits of controlled burns, which are destructive in the short term. Plants, insects, animals, and other parts of the ecosystem are destroyed or forced to flee to other places. If we only judged controlled burns by their short-term effects, most of us would never agree to move forward with such actions.

However, from a long-term perspective, controlled burns are very good for the health and vitality of the ecosystem. Plants come back stronger than ever, and the soil is enriched with nutrients that allow life to thrive. Controlled burns also create firebreaks that protect plant and animal life in the rest of the ecosystem should a wildfire break out.

In an effort to strengthen our environment and develop healthy ecosystems, many are asking how we can make the greatest impact. With limited resources at our disposal to improve our environment, along with limited time, we must be focused. We must define our goals and strategies clearly to be successful.

This focus is also necessary for corporate leaders. There are many options for growth, many ways to market your business, and many ideas to pursue, but you're restricted in these options by limited corporate resources. So what will you choose to do with those resources? Where will you invest your time? Where will you invest your money? Where will you direct the efforts and talents of your team? The answers to these questions are not always easy or obvious. Natural leaders are focused in order to use resources wisely. They attend meetings, participate in activities, and make use of resources only if they contribute to their goals. Other uses of resources may be promising, but they will turn them down if they do not fit with the overall objectives and priorities.

This focus does not come easily, for there are many good uses of your resources. There are charities that could benefit from your involvement, community boards on which to serve, meetings to attend, and people to contact. Managing resources wisely is not so much about efficiency as efficacy. Of course, efficiency is important, but if we're not effective—if we're not in touch with the imperatives that have profound impact on our organizations—everything else we do will be second-best.

Doreen Bolhuis, CEO of Gymco, is a great example of wise resource management. Bolhuis is certainly very efficient; she is organized and focused on the task at hand. Therefore, she always meets deadlines and accomplishes more than most people do in the course of the day or week.

However, what is more impressive is Bolhuis's effective leadership. She has built up her company so well that it continues to function even when she is absent. She stays focused on her priorities and is ready to say no to anything that does not support her vision. Bolhuis is known for asking insightful questions in meetings to determine the implications of a decision and how it will support her company's direction. As a result, Gymco is widely respected for the quality and depth of service it provides as a gymnastics education company.

Leaders often focus on actions that look good and assist the organization in the immediate future. The pressure they face to keep stockholders, staff, and clients happy is tremendous. While leaders know that their decisions may have negative implications down the road, they continue to respond to the urgencies of the moment in order to decrease their short-term stress. In effect, they are transferring their own pressures to the teams they lead, because their teams will be impacted the most by those negative implications.

For example, a company that I worked for in the past started to grow quickly and added more staff. It seemed that they were succeeding with a strong team that worked hard to reach goals. This success went on for a number of years. Eventually, management began to create incentives; many team members were promised bonuses and pay increases for meeting goals, and as a result, many worked hard and soon started to close in on their opportunity for rewards.

However, leaders within the organization began to get nervous about how many people were drawing bonuses because of the plan, and so they started to frequently change their compensation structure. In some instances, they claimed that the team merely misunderstood the intent of the plan, and in other instances, they said that they needed to "refine" the plan. The end result was that the staff became disillusioned with their compensation, and what began as a way to reward and motivate the staff ended up decreasing morale and trust.

As a leader, you will pay a price for any decision you make. But if you avoid paying the short-term, smaller price, the price you'll pay in the long term will increase exponentially. If you go into debt and postpone payment, the rules of compound interest ensure that you will pay much more in the long term. Therefore, the only question you face is, will you have the courage to make the right decision now, even if the benefits are not quickly realized? As a natural leader, you must cultivate a balanced perspective between short-term and long-term needs. If you follow the principles later outlined in chapter 6 for cultivating good relationships, then you will find it easier to muster the courage to stand in the gap and let your team know why your decisions are for the greater good.

Defining and evaluating success

Another way in which leaders use vision is to evaluate their success as an organization. There are many ways to define success, and without a clear definition, your evaluation will miss the mark. For example, you could decide your sales numbers will be the measure of your success. But if you're selling a lot of products while shortchanging your quality of service, you may also be losing customers. Therefore, if your vision as a company is to create raving fans, then strong sales numbers are an inaccurate measure of success; in terms of your vision, you have failed.

When we evaluate corporate success, we must be careful not to become enamored of financial gains and public recognition. Those factors are important, to be sure, but in the absence of progress toward implementing your vision, they are pointless. Others will see your claims of prosperity as shallow and lacking the meaning you defined in your vision statement.

One company in which this occurred had achieved tremendous growth within the first five years of its founding. Its leaders were adding staff on a regular basis and promised their team great financial rewards. Their reputation in the community grew, and they received several rewards for their growth.

However, their staff became disgruntled because, while they were receiving good pay, they had to work extremely long hours to succeed within the company. Talented staff started to burn out and leave, complaining to others in the community that they had not been appreciated by their supervisors. Even though they made money, these leaders were not achieving their vision of creating a great workplace that attracted the most talented and knowledgeable staff.

Truly successful companies define their success in light of how well their visions are being implemented and accomplished. They will spend time on a regular basis reviewing their visions to ensure that their goals and strategies support the directions they want to pursue. Natural leaders consistently use this definition of success, knowing that by doing so, they will ensure focus on their visions.

Assess Your Natural Leadership: Vision

1. Can you articulate and effectively communicate your vision?

2. How compelling is your vision? Does it excite you and your team?

3. How often are you integrating your vision into discussions?

4. How does your vision serve as a foundation for establishing priorities and departmental goals?

5. How do you define success? Does your definition reflect your vision?

Chapter 6:

Service to Others

Adam hesitated as he thought about his next question. He looked around again at the beauty surrounding him. "With so much work to do, how do you decide where to put your resources? After all, with this large ecosystem it must be costly and time-consuming to care for everything."

Ned smiled and said, "Why don't we sit over here under this palm tree?" Once seated, Ned continued, "You're right; it's difficult to know where to spend my time and resources. However, that picture becomes clearer when I stop to think about what is best for the ecosystem as a whole. I ask myself what will provide the best balance of nutrients, how the ecosystem can benefit the most people, and how we can do it in a way that fits with the needs of my team. The answer to those questions often sheds light on the right decisions."

In any ecosystem, attention must be paid to the needs of the plants, atmosphere, water systems, and soil. No part of the ecosystem has priority over the others; rather, they require a balanced coexistence. Each part of the ecosystem is interdependent, has equal value, and must be respectfully cared for. If any one of these components fails, all the rest are in jeopardy as well.

This equality between the different parts of natural ecosystems is true of corporate ecosystems as well. The most important lesson to draw from natural ecosystems is that leaders must look to balance the needs of those around them, not only their own needs. Natural leaders recognize the strength of interdependence and collaboration for the well-being of all concerned. They initiate processes and systems that will serve everyone's needs and allow both internal and external clients to thrive.

Creating a tri-focus

As a leader, you must maintain a balanced focus on the team, the client, and the organization. To serve clients well, you must create a team that is supported, resourceful, empowered, and capable of providing services. In order to do this, you must have a healthy organization and community. And to have a viable, profitable organization, you must focus on the needs of your clients. The three concerns are inseparable.

Some leaders are so busy taking care of their internal needs that they neglect the needs of those outside their organization. However, they realize all too soon that their clients have gone to their competitors, their alliances have dissolved, and the community at large is championing another robust, vital organization. Maintaining the balance between our internal clients (staff), external clients, and the community is at the forefront of natural leaders' minds. They understand that all three are essential for true success.

When leaders focus on others, they see results in excellent products and services. Natural leaders recognize that serving others means that they are continually striving to provide the best. You can never be satisfied with your efforts, or you will begin to make assumptions about what your internal and external clients need. Being self-satisfied prohibits you from effectively prioritizing your clients' desires and needs.

Excellence also demands that leaders provide quality in their products and services. Leaders who really care about clients will stand behind what they produce to avoid disappointing the customer. They will always strive for error-free products, services, and leadership. This commitment to quality control will permeate the staff, and they will recognize that the ways in which they work are just as important as the speed with which they complete tasks.

An example of this is Summit Landscape Management, whose owners are focused on the quality of products and services they provide. Mike Verhulst and Bill VanderVelde often will converse with staff about how to plant trees to provide the best view for the client, as well as how to use plants that are congruent with the landscape's environment. No detail is too small, and they diligently follow up with clients after a project is completed to ensure that everything met their expectations. This commitment to excellence has propelled them to be a preferred vendor for numerous Fortune 500 companies.

Another way in which your commitment to excellence affects your operations is through innovation. Innovation is impacted not only by your vision but also by your commitment to excellence. If you are striving for excellence, then by definition you will be involved in creating new solutions that meet new needs. The needs of those you serve are not static; therefore, you cannot be either. This drive will fuel your creativity as you develop new methods and techniques.

Innovation is not just about large-scale changes but also about changing ways of thinking, which is a part of our culture. Innovation can stem from external as well as internal sources. For example, the leaders of four noncompeting companies, Amway Corporation, Wolverine World Wide, Meijer, and Steelcase, have recently created a center for innovation called GRid70. Their leaders recognized the importance of innovation in their organizations, so they decided to put their design and product-development teams together in a center to foster innovative thought. Others from their organizations visit and hold meetings in the center to bring that same innovative spirit to their organizations as a whole.

Supporting staff

Natural leaders are motivated by serving the needs of others, whether they are internal team members or external clients. Natural leaders are goal-oriented and want to win whenever possible. But their goals always reflect the best interests of those they serve. They never forget that their successes lie not in making themselves look good, but rather in benefiting the people who follow them.

Nowhere is this more evident than when credit is given for a job well done. Many leaders tend to shine the light on themselves and the hard work they have done. In contrast, natural leaders step aside and shine the light on their team members. They know their successes can only be reached through the efforts of the entire team, not just themselves. While we all need praise from time to time, natural leaders are self-directed enough to provide their own internal praise and assessment of their performance.

Many organizations talk about being client focused. Leaders of such organizations put up mission statements about the client and discuss being client-centric at staff meetings. However, they fail to realize that, without an equal commitment to their staff members, these initiatives will fail.

Staff members will resent the fact that they lack the support and resources needed to do their jobs, while the majority of resources are being poured into keeping clients satisfied.

For example, a certain sales-driven organization consistently went to great lengths to satisfy its clients' interests and needs. They added new services, extended office hours to better service clients, and kept overhead to a minimum to keep prices low. Internally, they consistently talked about their clients' best interests.

However, that same level of attention was not given to staff. Management cut bonuses, expected staff to work many extra hours without reward, and constantly told staff that they just needed to work harder. This led to great frustration and burnout among team members. Within a six-month period, they experienced a 95 percent turnover. Needless to say, client service went down, and the leaders struggled to meet their organizational goals.

A very different example is that of Mike Novakoski, president of Elzinga & Volkers, a commercial construction and services company in the West Michigan area. They have a work force in the West Michigan area as well as employees across the country. Novakoski took the time to travel to one of their out-of-state facilities. This was not necessary, but he understood the importance of seeing his employees' work environment, talking with them directly, and communicating that they were important to the company. He used this and other trips to communicate his vision for the company and to encourage his team members to excel. As a result, there is tremendous loyalty to the company and to his leadership.

Novakoski has also continued to prioritize team building even during challenging economic times. He takes the team to Craig's Cruisers, a family amusement center, to relax and socialize. While this requires investment of time and dollars, he understands that providing this experience allows the team to work more effectively. He is focused on creating and supporting a strong team that can work together and anticipate the needs of internal and external clients. The results have propelled his company to the top of its industry.

Serving clients

Natural leaders seek to meet not only the needs of their staff, but also those of their clients. Being client focused requires diligence, a willingness to listen, and responsiveness to the client's needs. It requires leaders to walk in the shoes of their clients and see things from their viewpoint.

Therefore, natural leaders prioritize activities that create a strong focus on customer service. They will take the time to conduct customer surveys and to follow up after a project to ensure that the client's needs were met. Rather than relegating customer service to a department, natural leaders make sure that everyone shares the responsibility of ensuring customer satisfaction. They realize that everyone from the receptionist to the custodian to the president must be involved in customer service. Only when these objectives are integrated throughout your organization will your clients receive excellent customer service.

Consider the story of a doctor who went about his work efficiently. This doctor was very good at what he did and worked hard, but was not known for his bedside manner. One day, this doctor became ill and required a brief hospital stay. He went through the experience of being a patient, receiving medical tests, eating hospital food, and undergoing numerous examinations. By the end of his stay, his view of patient care had changed dramatically. He never viewed his patients the same way, and he was always sensitive to the feelings and needs of those under his care.

Contributing to community

Leaders make a commitment not only to their staff and to their clients, but also to the communities they serve. Green leaders seek to repay not only the people who have assisted them along the way but also the communities who patronize and support their organizations. Without this great system of support that successful leaders and companies enjoy, they could not grow, and their staff would not be drawn to work in their community. Therefore, community, as the third leg of the stool, is just as critical as staff and clients.

Leaders are grateful for mentors and coaches in the community who have helped them develop and hone their skills. They value the contribution that others have made in their journeys and want to give back as a way of saying thank you. Their humility underscores that people's success is never totally their own doing, but rather a result of everyone who has touched their lives.

Natural leaders give back in a number of ways. First, they mentor and coach others who are early in their careers. They may choose someone within their organization, but many times, they'll choose a promising young person in the community who they believe has potential to succeed. They remember how someone invested in them and continue that process for others.

They may also give back by donating time and financial resources for classes and seminars in the community. They may sponsor events that will create growth for young professionals. Many leaders also contribute to scholarship funds, knowing that the future of our community will rest in the hands of these young professionals.

Natural leaders view their communities as partners in their businesses and as resources to be nurtured. Out of great communities come great businesses, as well as thriving families and neighborhoods. Leaders seek to create stronger communities, since they know they are the foundations of their businesses. They also are grateful for the ways in which their communities have supported them and reciprocate that support.

This link between thriving organizations and thriving communities is very real and powerful. You only have to look at communities with high poverty and crime rates and poor-quality housing to see that businesses there soon decline and relocate. Strong communities attract more people, who in turn demand more goods and services. More workers then increase tax bases, which in turn provide more community services for businesses and others to enjoy. Organizational and community health are intertwined, and neither can be neglected.

In addition to understanding the link between community and organizational health, natural leaders genuinely care about others because it is the right thing to do. To reach out and help others is part of their DNA and values. Natural leaders prioritize activities that will have the greatest impact on the greatest number of people. Therefore, strengthening the community also becomes a consistent part of their strategy.

One such example is Bing Goei, president of Eastern Floral. He undertook a huge renovation project on an old building during the recent economic crisis to achieve three purposes. First, he wanted to obtain a building that would provide more space for his business and a better location for floral deliveries. Second, he wanted to do something that would benefit the neighborhood on the southwest side of Grand Rapids, Michigan. This area had been depressed, and developers had not invested much in that area. In contrast, Bing saw that this was a good location from which to do business. Third, he also wanted to provide office space for disadvantaged companies, so he planned to use approximately 10,000 square feet for their International Center for Entrepreneurial Excellence. He is also asking those companies to hire staff from the surrounding neighborhood. The impact Bing is having on that community is huge, and will be evidenced for a long time.

Creating win-win-win solutions

A leader's balanced focus is especially important in the area of problem solving. When seeking a win for everyone, the leader must maintain a threefold perspective in considering the impact on the organization, the team, and the client.

In fact, natural leaders have mastered the skill of creating great solutions based on this outer focus. Great solutions are based on a win-win-win philosophy. In essence, for a solution to be strong it has to meet three questions. First, will it benefit your clients? Second, will it benefit your staff? Third, will it benefit your organization? Much like a three-legged stool, your solution will not stand without support from all three areas; if the answer to any of these questions is no, then you do not have the best solution possible. Natural leaders take the extra time to brainstorm, problem solve, and work to find that balanced approach.

Many leaders' focus is clearly on themselves and their organizations. Their needs and wants are uppermost in their minds. While this allows them to succeed in the short term, they will pay a larger price in the long term. People are quick to see through their marketing materials to the truth of what is important to them.

I recently witnessed out-of-balance problem solving at a team meeting for a large transportation company. They had grown, but felt that they were not in touch with their clients' needs. Some of the relationships were not as strong as they needed to be, and so their team was developing new strategies to communicate more frequently and to strengthen their focus on the needs of the clients. The staff decided to brainstorm ways to accomplish this objective. The staff took ownership of the issue and seemed motivated to elevate their level of service. However, at one point in the discussion, one person asked, "I wonder how we can get our clients to fit in with our system?" Instead of asking how to change their current system, they wanted the clients to change to fit their own preferences.

Therein lies the problem. Leaders and managers are talking about serving clients, but are still trying to get them to conform to their organizational needs and systems. By definition, it will not work. Leaders cannot always require their clients or teams to change in order to fit their organization's needs. Instead, leaders must seek ways to meet the needs of their clients and teams. If leaders do this well, then their profitability will increase, productivity will rise, and client and employee retention will increase. All of this will result in a profitable and sustainable organization.

The good news is that, through additional training and guided discussions, the transportation company's staff began to see the difference between their beliefs and genuine customer service. The team caught the vision and began talking not only about changing systems to better fit the individual needs of their clients but also about changing even the physical surroundings for their clients. They paid attention to changing how customers were greeted when entering their facility, modifying posters on the wall to reflect the client's logo and business, and providing amenities that would show they were truly focused on their clients.

Assess Your Natural Leadership: Service

1. Does your definition of customer service focus only on external clients? Or does it include internal clients as well?

2. What have you done in the last six months to make raving fans of your team?

3. What are you willing to invest to see others succeed?

4. In what ways is your community a better place because of your organization?

5. Are your external clients' needs addressed even if it means a smaller sale for you?

Chapter 7:

Culture

Adam was astonished at Ned's response. "But how do you keep this ecosystem so vital? Most of the ones I've seen before are struggling with maintaining the right growing conditions. Many of their plants wither when the conditions are too hot or dry. But here, everything is so lush and green. How did you accomplish this?"

Ned looked around as Adam described what he saw. "Well, as a leader here, I have to protect our ecosystem and keep out anything that would endanger it. I also work with our team to ensure that they remember what is important in our environment and how to care for it. I take this part of my job seriously, knowing that if the environment is not healthy, the plants and animals will not thrive either.

"For instance, since we value nature and try to preserve our natural resources, we use as little water as possible. We collect rainwater, and only use it to water plants during cool times of day, so we don't lose moisture to the heat. We're very strict about this practice, as it ensures that our values are upheld."

Many areas of the earth have unique environments and ecosystems. If you took a trip around the world and visited Brazil, Russia, Africa, or any other area, you would experience very different environments, from the dry Sahara to the lush Amazon basin. Each and every climate is different. You experience the environment in every step that you take, in every scene that you observe. Even if no one described your environment to you, you would know about many of its qualities through your own experiences.

Likewise, each organization is permeated by a unique atmosphere and culture. It is unlike any other organization and will reflect a unique philosophy and set of values. Just like the physical environment of our planet, your internal culture is created by a combination of elements in your organization and leadership. This combination will continue to shape your culture as you grow.

Introducing values and philosophies

Many leaders mistakenly allow culture to develop on its own, rather than intentionally creating it around their vision and values. Allowing others to determine culture will put the organization at serious risk before it even gets started, as wrong elements and influences may then shape the organization's direction.

Instead, natural leaders introduce key philosophies and values into organizational culture. They will proactively determine the type of internal culture they want, and then infuse the culture with the needed ingredients. It's the same principle as planting a vegetable garden: if you want to grow beans, you would not go out and plant squash seeds, expecting to harvest beans. In a similar fashion, you must be sure to plant the kinds of seeds that will produce a healthy, thriving culture for your organization.

For example, if you want a highly collaborative culture, you should design an open facility with a large amount of meeting space, encourage teamwork on projects, and reward teams that produce new ideas. Your team will recognize that collaboration is a crucial part of your culture and begin to act accordingly. They will begin to seek each other out and look for ways to draw on each others' ideas and strengths.

As an example, I once worked with a large staffing company that successfully changed its cultural focus. It wanted to strengthen its staff's focus on teamwork, so it created weekly team contests. They posted the weekly contest on a dry-erase board, sometimes adding to the fun by creating a series of criteria on a tic-tac-toe grid. They measured how many new candidate interviews the team had completed, how many people the team had placed in jobs, and how many individuals had used the computer training center. This created a sense of fun for the staff and kept them focused on helping each other in order to win the prize at the end of the week. In this way, the company intentionally shaped the culture and kept the staff's focus on their vision.

As a result, the team was focused on those priorities and worked hard to ensure that they were reaching the goals. They consistently saw their efforts pay off, not only in terms of their weekly rewards, but also in terms of business growth, numbers of people employed, and even their own satisfaction in making progress toward these achievements.

Culture is built on your priorities for your company. By saying yes to one priority, you are saying no to another set of priorities. You are committing yourself to the things that matter most—not just the priorities you write down, but the priorities evidenced in how you spend your time and resources.

Therefore, if you spend a lot of time on customer service issues, your environment will reflect the importance you place on serving others. This priority will permeate your decision-making process, your meetings, and your projects with the thought of what is best for the client.

For example, a midsized firm was discussing growth strategies. They were aggressive in their efforts to grow the business, and had expanded rapidly from a local base to become a statewide and then regional company. This rapid growth was in large part due to their ability to penetrate large companies with multiple locations. They were succeeding by emphasizing their sales and marketing efforts. Therefore, they were rewarding their sales team with very expensive gifts that cost thousands of dollars. The sales people also had private offices and very flexible schedules.

On the other hand, the customer service and operations teams were given modest rewards for their work. Their bonuses were often in the hundreds of dollars, not thousands. Their schedules were somewhat flexible, but not nearly as lenient as the sales teams, and they were often called on to work very long hours.

As a result, the message to the staff was that, if you weren't in sales or directly impacting the bottom line, you weren't important. Therefore, there was huge turnover in the customer service department. Staff were brought in with great promises, but soon discovered that they were considered necessary cogs, not integral partners in the business. Morale sank, tensions grew between the two teams, clients were not served as well, and the erosion of their culture began.

Natural leaders understand that workplace cultures reflect not only their priorities but also their own attitudes. Our positive attitudes can create places in which people are fulfilled and challenged by their work as well as cultures that are creative and energized. For example, if you have a solutions-focused, can-do attitude, then your culture will display this same energy and forward thinking. If you maintain that attitude when challenges arise and there are no clear answers, then others in the organization will begin to learn to work through problems rather than be overwhelmed or crushed by them. They will instinctively be drawn to the same attitudes and behaviors that you are exhibiting.

As leaders, we must ask ourselves, "What attitudes am I displaying to my team? Are they positive and healthy attitudes, or negative and destructive?" Attitudes will grow and permeate your culture and environment. Just as wind and rain erode soil, a poor attitude will erode culture and leave it unable to sustain organizational life. Your organization will begin to lose talent and, ultimately, clients.

As a customer, you'll immediately notice the cultural attitudes of an organization. When you enter a retail store and hear the clerks complaining about their schedules or their wages, you know that the culture is not positive. Such negative attitudes undermine any energy that would contribute to growth. Not only are the staff unhappy with their work experiences but the clients are not being served. Staff with poor attitudes will not extend themselves to make others happy.

As a contrasting example, Jeff and Bill Bennett are two business leaders who exemplify the principle of positive returns for positive energy. They started a technical staffing company, called OtterBase, to provide talented workers in the IT, engineering, and scientific fields. The Bennetts are upbeat, energetic, and positive people. When you enter OtterBase's office, you are immediately greeted by a positive, outgoing staff member who seems really glad that you are there. You will see further evidence of this attitude as you walk through their offices and are greeted by other team members who are also positive and seem glad to welcome you.

This attitude has gone so far that the OtterBase staff has even created an acronym—PDH, which stands for "passion, diligence, and humility." This ethos has been so well integrated into the culture that staff will even sign off in an e-mail with "PDH." This might seem like a small gesture, but

59

it's indicative of the much larger way in which leadership at OtterBase has impacted the team and modeled this attitude and behavior for them.

In addition to the ways in which leaders' priorities and attitudes shape culture, there is a direct correlation between a leader's style and the development of organizational culture. For example, if yours is an informal, shared type of leadership, then it will be clear that power is not something to hold onto, but rather to share for the common good. As a result, staff will not engage in political maneuvering; instead, they will more quickly offer their assistance in leading projects and taking responsibility for additional tasks. They will have a stronger sense of working together and striving for common goals.

On the other hand, if your style is autocratic and staff members need your permission to act, they will not initiate. The culture will become rigid with rules telling people how to act and how to behave. Staff members will compete with each other for resources and promotions, all the while waiting to be told what to do. They will act only on the instructions they have been given. To do otherwise would be to risk disapproval and potential loss of position.

A rigid, hierarchical culture can create delays and extra costs. As an example, a certain legal firm that was well established and had offices throughout Michigan ended up with these sorts of problems through the culture created by its management committee. This committee would make decisions on everything, including hiring decisions, policies, and purchases. In fact, they were so involved in the day-to-day operations that no one could make a purchase without authorization if the cost was over fifty dollars. Therefore, almost all purchases and decisions were made within this committee.

This management style created such a bottleneck that decisions were usually delayed for about two months. Staff gave up on producing new ideas, since approval or rejection would take so long to obtain. Their motivation to develop and implement new ideas was gone as well. Micromanagement will always kill initiative and creativity in the workplace.

Another by-product of this management style was that the cost of each decision went up exponentially. Imagine the cost of five managers trying to decide on a fifty-dollar expense! The cost of our leadership style is great if we choose to cling to ineffective models.

Another example was shared with me by a business leader of a small company. He described how their president's micromanagement impacted their culture. He described the president's actions and leadership style as follows: "The president requires all the information to come to him. He feels that if he doesn't make the decision, then others won't do things correctly. The president feels it is his job to monitor each project and ensure that the team is following his lead."

Unfortunately, the result of his micromanagement is that the staff has shut down and is simply following a routine. They won't risk the president's disapproval by stepping out and trying something new. Consequently, the talented people have left, and the company is left solely with people who are willing to follow his lead. The culture has been weakened and demoralized through the president's leadership style.

Monitoring and renewing attitudes

We can learn a lot about how to guard our organizational cultures by looking at our current stewardship of the earth. We are currently surrounded by information and reports on the rapid decline of our environment. Scientists predict that if we continue using natural resources at our current pace, we will experience major ramifications on our lives and world within our lifetime. For example, we use fresh water at an alarming rate:

Ninety-seven percent of water on the Earth is salt water, and only 3 percent is fresh water of which slightly over two-thirds is frozen in glaciers and polar ice caps…the remaining unfrozen fresh water is mainly found as groundwater, with only a small fraction present above ground or in the air…Fresh water is a renewable resource, yet the world's supply of clean, fresh water is steadily decreasing. Water demand already exceeds supply in many parts of the world and as the world population continues to rise, so too does the water demand. Awareness of the global importance of preserving water for ecosystem services has only recently emerged as, during the 20th century, more than half the world's wetlands have been lost along with their valuable environmental services. [6]

Obviously we will face this and many other serious environmental issues, such as rising sea levels, flooding, and poor water quality, just

---

6   Wikipedia, "Earth's Water Distribution," accessed May 13, 2009, http://en.wikipedia. org/wiki/File:Earth%27s_water_distribution.svg.

to name a few, in the near future if world leaders do not address these concerns. Natural leaders know that poor attitudes like oil slicks in the environment spread and infect the entire culture (ecosystem).

In the corporate world, it's equally important to guard our "natural resources"—our culture. The difference is that culture is something we *create*, and it's renewable through instilling a system of checks and balances. Like the natural world, culture is not static and is constantly changing in either a positive or negative way. Since your culture is changing, you need to monitor, measure, and ensure the changes are moving in a positive direction in order to protect your staff, clients, and organization from harmful influences.

Only you as a leader can create and then guard your culture. This is not an area that can be delegated to anyone else, since the results are so critical for the sustainability of your organization. Your organization will rise and fall with the focus and priority you give to this essential area.

A quick way to identify the health of your organization is to ask yourself, "How many complaints and problems do I hear in a day? In a week?" Leaders commonly lament that they are always putting out fires. If this is true, what does this communicate about your culture? People typically complain in an attempt to reconnect with leaders they feel are out of touch; they're signaling that they feel they are not heard, or that they are not valued for their contributions. Of course, there are exceptions, but they are just that—exceptions. When your culture is strong, full of vision, and rewarding to those who work hard and demonstrate respect, then problems are more readily resolved. Instead of constantly complaining, people will focus on working together to find solutions.

If your organization suffers from poor attitudes among staff, lethargy, or lack of ownership, you can be sure these issues stem from a weak culture. Strong leaders will detect and remove these attitudes from their organizational cultures, not allowing them to take root. You must pay attention to the smallest things that can undermine your priorities. When inappropriate elements are present, corrective action is required.

Guarding against internal and external pressures

A natural leader pays attention to the attitudes, philosophies, and perspectives brought into the work environment and takes corrective action when needed. Your culture is similar to the air you breathe. If the air becomes polluted, you begin to cough and wheeze, and your health fails. Likewise, a culture will begin to crumble when poor attitudes, disrespect, and disharmony are present.

Strengthening your culture will require analyzing the root cause of its issues. Many leaders treat symptoms rather than root causes, and so the same problems arise again in different guises. Natural leaders ensure that they have identified the root cause, even if the cause stems from their leadership. Looking for patterns in past behaviors and actions will usually assist in this process. For instance, if you believe that one department is the cause of your problems, then look deeper before you start formulating a solution. On deeper reflection, you may find consistent conflict in multiple relationships, silos between multiple departments, and lethargy in numerous team members. This will then signal that the issue is deeper than just one department's problems.

Once you have identified the root cause, you must take corrective action. This can be anything from removing a staff member who persists in behaving counterproductively to recasting vision with the team to ensure their focus and priorities represent the values of the organization. Reviewing the questions at the end of each of the chapters in this book is a good place to start identifying the appropriate corrective action. The answers to these questions will begin to highlight where you are weakest and where renewed attention and effort on your part will make the greatest impact.

Guarding culture is more than monitoring the sum of your employees' internal attitudes; you must also be alert to such external pressures as market shifts, client demands, and financial instability. While we cannot control many of the factors in our communities and markets, we can take steps to minimize the impact of those issues on the organizations we serve.

In particular, external financial pressures can greatly impact your culture. When you are overextended with debt, banks are more reluctant to loan you additional money to fuel your growth. This type of pressure is felt throughout the organization and pulls your staff's attention away from your values and philosophy and toward getting sales up. Staff will begin to ignore quality issues and instead focus on speed and profitability. While this helps in the short term, it will erode your relationships with clients and be self-defeating in the end.

Always keep in mind that, while pressure may seem to be external (e.g., banks refusing to lend additional funds to your company); the real threat was created by your decision making. The decision to extend yourself financially and enter into heavy debt set the stage for a more significant impact on your organization. As a leader, you must not place your organization at risk; you must protect your culture from as many external distractions as possible.

Another external pressure organizations face is market shifts. As clients demand change, technology develops, and new innovations are introduced, the market will shift. Your organization will then feel the impact of those industry and market shifts and will be forced into making costly changes to keep pace. The cost of incorporating new technology or new products and services can be expensive, but it is essential to obtaining and keeping clients.

Again, the pressure may *seem* external, but bear in mind that its source is also internal: your team did not proactively anticipate these changes. Or maybe your team *did* foresee the changes, but did not adequately prepare staff and processes to service those emerging needs. Therefore, much of your focus and resources are poured into *catching up* to the changes that have emerged. Unfortunately, in doing so you become so focused on reacting that you give up other values, such as quality, customer service, and forward thinking. You are forced to abandon other growth initiatives to shore up your market presence, and in so doing, you weaken the organization.

The printing industry's response to external pressures over the last five to ten years illustrates the dangers of merely "reacting." Many printing companies felt that they would always have a large market. So they continued to invest heavily in printing presses and other equipment. However, with advances in technology, their client companies started to print their own materials internally. Computer software and printers advanced to the point that anyone could run multicolor pieces on demand. This market shift caused a fairly rapid decline in the need for external printing services.

As a result, margins dropped, volume dropped, and profitability for most printing companies dropped. Many went out of business. Why? Most failed to look forward soon enough to respond to the changes in their industry and market. They were left with expensive, unused equipment, decreased sales, and little idea of how to reverse the trend. The real threat became a lack of focus on the things that allowed them to succeed in the first place, which included responsiveness to clients, creating a professional image, and building strong relationships with their clients.

An example of a printing company that has bucked this trend is Allegra Print & Imaging. President Eric Vetter realized early on that the industry was significantly changing, but was not sure how to respond. Through a great deal of brainstorming and careful planning, his company decided to expand their printing services beyond mechanical presses. Today they use digital printing presses and computers to create high-quality plates and produce images at an affordable price.

Allegra Print & Imaging has also expanded its services beyond printed paper products, now including promotional products and direct mailings. They are involved in the planning and design phases, the actual printing, and the copyrighting aspects of a project. From beginning to end, they are providing full-service marketing to their clients at a very attractive price point. Rather than being left behind, they are at the forefront of their industry.

Natural leaders always vigilantly monitor and protect their organizations. They seek to prepare their organizations so as to limit the impact of outside pressures. One such example is Porter Hills Retirement Communities & Services, which provides numerous services to the senior population. One of the market trends that their president, Larry Yachcik, observed and is proactively directing his team to respond to is that most seniors today wish to avoid living in assisted care facilities. They fervently desire to stay in their homes and enjoy their independence. Therefore, Porter Hills is invested in technology and services that help seniors remain in their homes and is emphasizing its home health care division. These two steps, along with person centered strategies, are positioning Porter Hills to serve seniors in their homes, taking advantage of a mindset and potential trend that is counter to the forty-year history of providing housing and services in a congregate setting. These two steps, along with other strategies, will position them to serve seniors' demand for independence, taking advantage of a trend that could have been a negative impact on their bottom line.

Assess Your Natural Leadership: Culture

1. When you list your top priorities, do they support your values?

2. When evaluating your last few decisions, are they congruent with your philosophy and values?

3. On an average week, how many complaints do you make in front of your team?

4. What does your organization's culture suggest about your leadership style?

5. How is your leadership style benefitting your organization, and how is it hindering the organization?

Part III:
Mastery of Team

Chapter 8:

Hiring

Adam and Ned stood, stretched their legs, and walked further down the path. They quietly viewed the various plants and waterways as they passed. Finally Adam said, "You have so many different plants and species here. How do you decide what to bring in and how much to plant? It must be overwhelming!"

"Yes," said Ned. "It can be a bit challenging. However, whenever we are deciding which plants or species to bring in, we look to our environment and identify the kinds of plants that would work best in our ecosystem. Not every plant will thrive here.

"For example, one time we mistakenly brought in a flowering plant that needed constant care and attention. For it to grow and do well, we needed to pick off the dead blooms and water it almost daily. We're not equipped to provide that much attention. Therefore, the plant withered and died. So, we've learned to spend more time considering which plants really fit with our environment and resources."

Today, environmentalists encourage people to select native plants for their gardens and landscapes. By doing so, they ensure that the plants will grow well in their region, fit well with the ecosystem, and not overshadow other inhabitants, invade their spaces, or introduce new diseases. Selecting native plants ensures harmony and balance among species. On the other hand, poor selection will result in lost resources and frustration and will negatively impact the environment.

The same is true for leaders as they make decisions about hiring new employees. You must consider how a person will fit with your culture, your vision, and your team. Poor hiring decisions will negatively affect not only the person you hired but also your culture. Poorly matched people will leave a "carbon footprint" which will negatively impact your organization's culture, making it difficult to attract the most talented staff. Just as certain plants will only grow well in certain conditions and soils, employees need certain types of cultures and environments to thrive. Some people will thrive in an open and creative environment, while others will thrive in a more structured, systems-oriented organization. Your culture determines who should be selected to ensure a great fit with your team and mission.

Assessing values

One of the ways in which you find out if potential employees would be good fits for your culture is by identifying their values. Probe them in the job interview to understand more about how they think and what is important to them, for these two components will determine the actions and behaviors that drive their work and predict their success.

First let's look at how people think and make decisions. You can uncover this by asking "why" questions. For example, "Why did you select the college or university you attended? Why did you go into sales?" Their responses will speak volumes about their thought processes. For example, suppose someone responds that she went to a school because it was close to home, or because all her friends were going there. It would seem that she makes decisions based on what is easiest and follows the crowd rather than thinking through what would be best for her. In taking the path of least resistance, she has not learned to initiate, be independent, or look at the long-term impact of her decisions. The answer to these questions will also begin to demonstrate how a candidate will act in the future. If she followed the path of least resistance in the past, you can be sure that she will probably do so again.

Even asking a candidate why she is interested in your position will produce insights. I have heard such candidate responses as "It's close to home," "It sounds like something I could do," or "My aunt used to work here." None of these reasons are bad in themselves, but if that is the only reason a candidate can think of, she will leave as soon as there is a job opening even closer to home.

However, if the candidate were to respond, "My passion is to ensure quality in the products I provide to clients, and I know that your company has a great reputation for producing quality goods," or "I love to resolve issues for clients and turn an angry client into a positive client," she will probably be a strong addition to your company. Both responses are strong examples of how she demonstrates her interest in your position and the work she would be doing. You always want to look for someone who is interested in the actual work.

Also pay attention to candidates' attitudes toward life, work, and their previous supervisor. Do they have positive attitudes toward life and work? This may seem like an insignificant consideration, but it is fundamental to any person's or organization's success. A positive attitude will allow prospective employees to overcome obstacles and focus on solutions, not problems. You can be sure that, instead of being crushed by the obstacles, they will look for a path around challenges.

In addition to a positive attitude, candidates' expectations toward the organization and supervisor are critical. For example, if candidates expect that supervisors are there to tell people what to do, that will begin to permeate their approach to work. They won't be interested in taking initiative, but will instead perform the routine tasks required to collect their paychecks. You will need to spoon-feed them each step of a task, and they will resist volunteering for anything extra.

For example, a manager in a large human service agency was responsible for supervising ten staff members and overseeing the client services of his department. He'd been with the organization for some time and had developed a strong sense of loyalty. The agency was growing rapidly and taking on new initiatives, and as more clients were acquired, the workload grew. Everyone had to become more efficient, be willing to initiate, and put in longer hours.

However, this manager was reluctant to take on anything new. He did his accustomed tasks well, but when faced with new tasks would say he was busy and wait for others to volunteer. If his supervisor specifically asked him to do something, he would agree, but would not always follow through.

He was also determined not to work any more hours than needed. The organization had created job descriptions that clearly stated that managers were expected, on average, to work forty-five hours. This individual, therefore, came in at 7:00 a.m. and worked until 5:00 p.m. He was putting in his forty-five hours, but no more. This was frustrating to his peers, who were sometimes working fifty-five hours each week. There was a mismatch between his "punch in and punch out" attitude and the organization's new needs for ownership and initiative.

One of the questions you can ask to determine candidates' expectations toward their supervisors is "Tell me about the best supervisor you worked for in the past." In answering this question, they will tell you quite a bit about their expectations and attitude toward the person who will oversee their work. Some candidates might respond, "We got along great and even went shopping after work," "They were always around to solve problems for me," or "They allowed me to have a flexible schedule." Again, while there is nothing wrong with these answers, they may not match your views of what a supervisor should provide. These answers tend to focus on supervisors who provide friendship, do the hard work for their employees, or who allow employees to prioritize their personal above their professional lives. If you are looking for someone to bring energy, passion, and innovation to the position, these answers may be indicative of a bad fit.

Watch for realistic and positive answers about their experience with supervisors. For instance, if candidates state, "My supervisor was willing to provide training and allow me to grow," or "They provided me with needed resources and empowered me to use them in resolving issues," these answers speak more to how their supervisors supported and empowered them, rather than taking over employees' problems and responsibilities.

You must also examine candidates' attitudes toward teamwork. For some people, teams just slow them down and get in the way of what they want to accomplish. Therefore, these people will be resistant to anything that is important to the team but does not seem to help them accomplish their personal goals. They will find ways to miss team meetings, avoid sharing information with the team, and decline invitations to team events.

Two very different examples demonstrate the tremendous impact this principle has within your organization. The first example is of a company that upheld their team values in their hiring practice. EduTek Midwest provides technology and learning solutions for educators. They were seeking additional team members and interviewed a candidate with a reputation as a rainmaker for a sales position. Everything they knew about this person clearly indicated that he was very good at opening doors and obtaining sales. However, when meeting with this candidate, it became clear to them that he was not interested in being part of a team. He wanted to be left alone to accomplish his goals and did not want to communicate with or assist others on the team. Ultimately, they decided not to hire this individual, since his values were in opposition to theirs. Inevitably, this candidate would have eroded their culture and created dissension within the team.

As a contrasting example, I once consulted for a small but growing firm that decided to ignore the conflicting values of a certain employee. This employee was their best salesperson and had been with them for a few years, but was not highly thought of by the team. In interviews with the team about the organization's strengths and challenges, this individual's name came up consistently as someone they were concerned about. When I further questioned their concerns, it became apparent that this person saw himself as apart and isolated from the team, and that his values were not congruent with those of the rest of the organization. In order to gain more sales, this individual would enter gray areas legally and ethically.

Upon concluding my interviews, I gave my assessment back to the organization, and I asked management about this individual. They responded by telling me what a great salesperson he was and how he was always at the top in reaching his quotas. They knew that he had some issues, but they assured me that they were keeping close tabs on him and that they felt he was contained in his activities. So, despite my reservations, they seemed comfortable allowing things to continue as they were.

About two months after this conversation, I discovered that the individual in question had ignored policy and industry regulations in his zeal to close a sale. This infraction became a disaster for the organization. They almost lost their largest client, were faced with potentially huge fines, and could have lost their license. Top management spent countless hours cleaning up the havoc. And all this was brought about by an individual whose values were clearly different from the organization's.

People who think they are "above" the team are dangerous to both cultures and organizations. They will often resist being held in check by their supervisors or taking input from the team. They most certainly will not seek to share their insights with others and will view such activity as a waste of time. If they figure out how to succeed, they feel everyone else should succeed as well, without any help from them. Their sole focus is on their own success, instead of on that of the team or the organization as a whole.

Identifying highly talented people

Most employers will begin their recruiting and hiring process by reviewing the job description, defining the skills needed to succeed, and then creating interview questions that will identify whether or not those skills are present. This practice seems very logical, and will in fact assist the department where the person will serve.

However, in the long run it will prove limiting if applicants are hired solely on the basis of their current skills. While it is important to identify the underlying skills needed to succeed in the job, a more crucial consideration is the applicants' talents. For example, if you're hiring an administrative assistant, you might very well focus on how fast applicants can type, the computer programs they've mastered, and so forth. This might predict how efficiently applicants will complete assignments, or how well they'll be able to use your current computer system. However, if the programs they use or the duties they perform change, will they be able to adapt their skills and experiences? If they are not talented, all the other skills they possess will eventually limit them.

Talent is defined by *Webster's* as "a characteristic feature, aptitude, or disposition of a person; the natural endowments of a person; a special, often creative or artistic, aptitude." Talent surpasses skill in that it defines a person's capacity to perform, grow, and use those same skills in new ways. When new problems and challenges arise, talented people can craft new solutions by applying former experiences, skills, and knowledge. They can see beyond the actual steps of what they are doing to understand the deeper issues. Their approach to new situations is creative and innovative.

Talent allows people to grow with your organization and meet future as well as present needs. When you hire based on skill, you are hiring for today's needs, for the short term. This strategy will not serve you well in the future; organizational environments change so quickly these days that as soon as we master something, we will need to begin learning new approaches to accomplish the same or other objectives. Talent supports and enhances individuals' ability to use skills in many different settings and projects.

Another way to recognize talent is to identify a candidate's passion for growth. Talented employees are drawn by experiences that will stretch them and provide opportunities to learn. They enjoy testing their skills in new situations and are confident in taking on new projects. This desire to learn allows them to be teachable and learn from the insights and wisdom of others. Individuals who are teachable will always surpass people who think that they have everything figured out because by remaining open to new ideas, they are allowing the cultivation of innovative thoughts that will spark creativity and permit them to excel.

This desire and capacity to learn can be readily identified in the interview with well-thought-out questions. For example, you might ask, "What is one new thing you learned in your last position? What new skills do you hope to learn in our position? What tools do you use to continue learning about your profession?" Their responses will tell you a lot about their attitude toward learning and their commitment to professional growth.

An individual who exemplifies this concept is Marlin Feyen, president of Feyen Zylstra, a leading Midwest electrical contractor. Feyen has worked in the industry for many years; however, his love of learning has never ceased. He has continued to take classes, not only in his own industry but also in such diverse areas as astronomy, Spanish, and energy trends. For Feyen, learning is just a part of life, and one that he relishes as he looks to the future.

Feyen's commitment to his own and his employees' learning furthers his company's professional growth. Feyen Zylstra continues to expand even in challenging economic times. For example, by improving his understanding of international issues, Feyen has prepared himself to serve clients globally. As another example, by "loaning" out his employees to area nonprofits on a regular basis, Feyen helps his team learn new skills and share existing skills with community agencies. Employee morale is on the rise, and clients receive valuable service from his team.

Creating balanced teams

After thirteen years of consulting and working with leaders on hiring practices, I'm amazed by how many times I've heard leaders say, "I really like Joe or Mary as a candidate." What they are really saying is that they would like these candidates as friends or acquaintances. While it is wonderful to feel that you enjoy another person's conversation, this is hardly the basis for making a good hiring decision.

In fact, it could very well be the reason that you should *not* hire that person. For example, we often like people who seem to share our work styles and strengths. However, if you are hiring someone who needs to perform duties and responsibilities that are not your strengths, then it stands to reason that you will need to hire someone whose behavioral style is very different from yours.

Another important way of incorporating diversity into your team is to hire people with different life and work experiences. Avoid the trap of hiring only from one college or from a certain type of company. In doing so, you'll gain fresh ideas and techniques for your products and services. This is important because, with time, our perspective on our own company can become blurred. If you've ever needed reading glasses, you can understand this process intuitively. You might have spent your entire life reading letters and numbers just fine, but if your vision deteriorates, those same figures will no longer appear as they really are. Therefore, much as obtaining a prescription for glasses improves our eyesight, hiring people with diverse life and work experiences brings correction to our organization "sight." These new hires do not assume that our methods are the best or only way to accomplish goals. They question our systems and techniques and ask many more questions than employees who have been there for a number of years. Their fresh eyes cause us to rethink our assumptions.

The rich, intricate tapestry of ideas and perspectives that diversity creates is invaluable. It is out of these diverse perspectives that you strengthen your products and services and separate yourself from your competitors.

Diversity presents tremendous opportunities for leaders and organizations. Team diversity brings opportunities in the form of new ideas, greater capacities to achieve, and new strengths within the team. This blending creates excitement, creativity, and synergy to produce the best solutions and ideas. Client services have the potential to reach new heights based on these diverse attributes.

It is truly awe-inspiring to watch a well-matched yet diverse team work together. It is like visiting a conservatory that is full of rich colors and different types of foliage. You are immediately drawn to such a conservatory, and as you linger you notice the shapes, scents, and textures of an incredible number of plants. As you observe the details, you notice new scenes emerging, almost like a play unfolding. Likewise, a diverse team can take you on unexpected, rich, and creative paths.

When strong leadership is in place, leaders can identify people's talents and exercise wisdom in avoiding people who will invade or destroy their healthy culture. In other words, they spend considerable effort in the hiring process to ensure that employees will further support the culture and values of the organization.

Assess Your Natural Leadership: Hiring

1. How are you identifying a candidate's values and work philosophy during the interview?

2. How much time do you spend during orientation talking about your vision, values, and culture?

3. If someone is not a good match with your values and philosophy, do you still hire them to fill the position quickly?

4. Are the attitudes of your employees tied to your evaluations and compensation or bonus process?

5. How long after identifying a wrong fit does it take you to remove a team member?

Chapter 9:

Communication

As Adam considered what Ned had shared, he asked, "How do you and your team stay in touch? It seems like the ecosystem is so large and you must be so busy getting work done. How can you communicate with one another?"

Nodding, Ned said, "That has been a problem. At first I thought that once my team knew what they needed to get done, I could just walk away and it would be fine. But when the team didn't hear from me for a while, they lost focus and didn't remember why what we are doing here is so important. I found that more problems erupted when they felt I didn't care.

"So now we have regular meetings before our days begin to share what we are seeing and what challenges we are experiencing. We hear the excitement when things are succeeding, and can encourage one another when they are struggling. Many times the team will bring up issues that I haven't even discovered yet. This meeting time has become so valuable to me I wouldn't miss it for the world!"

Sometime when you are out in nature, stop and just listen. At times it will seem quiet and very still, but gradually as you listen, you will hear birds calling to each other, crickets chirping, and other quiet background sounds. All of these sounds are nature's way of communicating.

Communication is common to many living things and yet is unique to each creature within nature. Each species has its own unique "language." For example, even though most humans can't understand a robin's chirps, other robins gain vital information about activities, needs, and threats from those sounds.

Likewise, as a leader, your communication skills must be honed to fit the people you want to impact and lead. In order to be effective, leaders know that they must vary their style. The central message will be the same, but the delivery of that message may be very different. Natural leaders initiate changes in their style, instead of waiting for team members to change their own styles to fit those of leaders.

Listening actively

You can identify necessary changes in your communication style by actively listening to and observing people as you speak with them. Many leaders focus on their words, tone, and methods of communicating information to another person. However, natural leaders understand that listening is the beginning of all strong communication.

Listening is often regarded as unimportant, since it seems like a nonproductive activity. You become restless and eagerly wait for your turn to tell the other party your thoughts and solutions. Therefore, many leaders resist listening in favor of activity and speech. But in spending their energies crafting what they wish to say next, they miss extremely valuable information.

True listening is active and engages all of your senses in understanding the spoken and unspoken needs of the other party. It is through this active listening that you gain valuable insights into what is important to others and how they think about the project or issues you are discussing.

For example, a vice-president of human resources for a large manufacturing company described to me his techniques for entering into negotiations with their labor union. Most union negotiations have a reputation for being contentious and loud. This gentleman took a very different approach from others in his field. He would start out by listening to the union's perspective and asking enough questions so that he really understood their viewpoint. In fact, he would strive to understand and present their perspective better than *they* could. Notice that this was his first priority, before he ever presented management's proposal. Only after this was accomplished would he begin to respond with management's perspective.

His second unusual tactic was to lower his voice to a quiet level. This necessitated that the union representatives listen quietly and closely to what he was communicating about management's proposal. It was amazing how this simple technique changed the dynamics of what had traditionally been a very anxious and aggravating exchange. Instead, both sides were able to have calm and productive exchanges of ideas. The vice-president was able to present management's proposal in light of the union's concerns and needs, creating a win-win resolution. His reputation for being a leader grew, because he excelled in his communication skills and therefore was very successful in developing strong relationships with those in the labor union.

As you can see from this example, listening involves actively probing what is said and not said and attempting to gain insights. How do leaders know what their teams are thinking? They listen. The information gained then becomes the basis for deciding how to share information and your vision with the team. Listening creates the opportunity to understand, formulate, and appropriately respond to others.

Listening, in fact, is one of the most powerful tools you have as a leader. It demonstrates respect to other people and engages them in your vision and solutions. Natural leaders know that mastering the art of listening is critical if they wish to become effective communicators. Only those who develop the ability to listen will earn the right to be heard by those they serve.

Adapting communication styles

Just as every species communicates through different sounds, movements, colors, or even chemicals, humans also have different communication styles. Mostly, when you communicate, you do not stop to think about how you are going to say something; you just go ahead and say it in the way that seems most comfortable and sensible to you.

However, you will observe that some people talk faster than others, some ask more questions, some give broader perspectives and ignore details, and still others give lengthy explanations filled with details. This works great when we are talking to those who have preferences and styles similar to ours. However, when we are talking to counterparts with very different styles or preferences, our communication can create confusion and misunderstanding. Consider the following statement and the implied meaning created by placing the emphasis on different words:

I never said she lied about the accident.

I *never* said she lied about the accident.

I never *said* she lied about the accident.

I never said *she* lied about the accident.

I never said she *lied* about the accident.

I never said she lied about the *accident.*

You have said the same words, but the meaning has changed dramatically based on where you placed the emphasis. Now multiply that change in meaning by the different words, tone of voice, and nonverbal gestures used. You can imagine the number of miscommunications that happen all the time due to these variables. Therefore you must be attuned to individuals and their preferences, rather than relying on what seems natural to you. It may feel awkward at times, but mastering and adapting your style and presentation will pay huge dividends.

This does not mean that you change the message you deliver. The content of your information must reflect your true feelings and ideas. However, the manner in which you communicate that information will change based on other people's communication and behavioral styles. This adaptation is powerful and will minimize miscommunication.

For example, have you ever listened to someone talk so fast that you gave up trying to keep pace with the conversation, instead merely nodding when it seemed appropriate? Or maybe the person was droning on about endless detail, and you found your mind wandering to other topics, only to realize that they had moved on to another topic without you noticing. These are real-life experiences that happen to all of us at some point and leave us wishing we could end the conversation quickly.

A more positive example would be when someone matches your pace and uses a style that is in sync with yours. It feels easy and very comfortable to exchange information with that person. You feel you're speaking your natural "language." You find yourself enjoying the conversation and becoming energized by it.

Adapting your communication style not only avoids miscommunication but also demonstrates respect. When you extend yourself by listening and recognizing individual preferences, you send a very powerful message: that you care about employees and their needs, which is the foundation of strong relationships. Only then will others extend themselves and follow your lead.

John Maxwell, a national author and speaker on leadership, puts it this way: "People don't care how much you know, until they know how much you care."[7] As a leader, you can never overestimate the truth of this statement. The way in which you communicate will speak volumes about how much you care for those you are leading, and about how far you are willing to stretch yourself for their benefit.

In addition to changing their styles, natural leaders use communication techniques to highlight and reinforce their values and philosophies. They understand that telling people about their values a single time or in a single way is never enough. In fact, natural leaders look for multiple ways to communicate this vital information to their team. They use every opportunity to underscore the central focus and the priorities for the organization.

For example, natural leaders will often tell stories of past situations to communicate their values, such as honesty and service to others. Using a story in which honesty was displayed, or when clients were well served, makes a tremendous impact on the listener. From that story, listeners will learn how to apply that value or philosophy, and they are far more likely to remember what you have told them than if you simply state the information. Your team may not remember every word of a mission statement you put on the wall of your lobby. They will, however, remember a "word picture" (story) that teaches them how to act and make decisions in the future.

Stories are so powerful because they bridge the gap between emotions and logic to engage the entire person. Stories are compelling and cause the team to remember and embody your philosophy. As you tell these stories, you'll prompt your team to act on the very concepts and principles that you care so deeply about.

A story can be dramatic, like my earlier anecdote about the grocer throwing out tainted fruit, or it can be much more understated. For instance, you could share a story about how you persevered through obstacles early in the life of your business, and the lessons you learned through that experience. Whatever story you tell, make sure it communicates the principle you want team members to learn, and relate it so as to fit your listener's communication style.

---

7   John Maxwell, *The 21 Irrefutable Laws of Leadership* (Nashville: Thomas Nelson Publishers, 1998), 107.

You can never tell your team too often what you care about, for without reinforcement, time erodes the impact of our message. You can do so through striking up conversations, sharing articles in newsletters, books, or blogs, putting inspirational quotes or information in people's paycheck envelopes, and many other creative means. If you think about it, there are so many ways to saturate your culture with this information that there should never be a reason for your team to forget or lose sight of these imperatives.

For example, Mike Verhulst, president of Summit Landscape Management, writes quotes on a dry-erase board in the company's conference room. Sometimes, he will write a single word, such as "perseverance." Other times, he may write down a full quote, such as "Be decisive even if it means sometimes you'll be wrong," "Know that happiness is not based on possessions but on your relationships with the people you love," or "Become the most positive and enthusiastic person you can." He usually will add an event of the day to the saying to personalize it or describe how it pertains to Summit. He knows that as people read those quotes, they'll pause and think about the ways in which they go about their work. These quotes range in topic, but they all reinforce important values and themes that will guide his staff as they make decisions about their work.

Selling, not telling

Natural leaders also make use of the critical principle of selling, not telling, in their communication styles. Natural leaders do not need to use positional authority in their communication. Rather than demand that their teams do something because they are the boss, they are able to persuade others based on who they are as people. This persuasive power is based on the trust and depth of their relationships with their teams. Team members understand that leaders are working for the good of everyone, and therefore are willing to follow their lead.

For example, I recently heard Terri Kelly, president and CEO of W. L. Gore & Associates, speak as part of a leadership conference. W. L. Gore employs nine thousand associates in thirty countries and produces a wide range of products. At a conference, Kelly described their very unique approach in selecting leaders. She said that their teams actually vote for who they want to lead them. Therefore, leaders know that they must demonstrate the right to lead by developing strong relationships and influencing the projects and direction the team will work on together.

This approach affirms the reality that leadership is a privilege, and one that is created by the strength of relationships. These leaders are not running around putting out fires and telling people what to do. Instead, Kelly went on to describe that leaders seek to bring fresh ideas and use persuasion to gain support for new projects they want to launch. This type of collaboration between teams and leaders is helping their company grow by leaps and bounds.

When you have hired the right people and are regularly communicating your values and philosophy to the team, staff can then be motivated to persevere and work through the challenges they face. When people start new jobs, they are usually excited and highly motivated to work hard and to learn their new roles. Over time, though, they tend to settle into a daily routine, and their energy levels can drop off to a maintenance mode. Challenges can become more daunting, and the negatives of their days feel more cumbersome.

When you regularly communicate with your team and remind them of the importance of what the organization is accomplishing, it compels them to keep their energy high and to push through the challenges they face. Communicating your vision and mission is a key to ensuring that your teams do not just maintain their level, but rather excel daily.

Every conversation, every meeting, every decision, and every situation in which you become involved is an opportunity to motivate the team. Natural leaders are always aware of this and make use of these opportunities to engage people and to call them to action. When you communicate appropriately, people become engaged in the creation and implementation phases, knowing that the outcome will be exciting and important.

People are far more motivated when they are committed to something that is bigger than them; something they care about and that they know will impact the organization and those they serve. Show me someone who is unmotivated, and I will show you someone who has lost sight of why they come to work. Money will not do it, nor will threats.

Doreen Bolhuis, president and founder of Gymco, said recently in a presentation to a business group, "You can demand that people show up to work as a result of obtaining a paycheck. But you cannot demand that people give you their very best creativity and work. That is a gift. A gift they have to freely give to you."

What motivates people to give that gift? Daniel Pink, in his recent book *Drive*, talks about the incredible power of purpose. Purpose gives people a reason to be engaged, a reason to get out of bed on Monday morning, and a reason to give all of their talents and creativity to their work. [8] This purpose comes from leaders who use every opportunity to talk about purpose, vision, and direction.

Resolving conflict quickly

Any time more than one person is involved in a project, there will be conflict. Teams that work well with one another must be able to resolve these conflicts quickly and reach effective resolutions. Conflict, if resolved well, can actually strengthen teams and allow them to find better solutions.

Think about that statement again. Conflict can actually strengthen team relationships and foster better solutions. How? Conflict is not inherently bad, but rather causes you to re-examine your thoughts, ideas, and assumptions. It is through this examination that you will uncover flaws and gain new perspectives, leading to better processes and outcomes.

Therefore, you must fight the inclination to ignore conflicts and issues that arise within your team. Ignoring conflicts will result in many problems, the largest being that the issue will not go away. It will in fact grow larger and spill over into all sorts of areas, draining your staff's energy, focus, and time.

For example, a midsized company in the Midwest was struggling with a conflict between two employees that had been going on for eight years. Since the conflict had been going on for a long time, people who were not originally part of the conflict had taken sides, and the entire department had dissolved into all kinds of petty arguments. The cost to this organization was huge in terms of lost productivity and distractions. The top executives had tried several unsuccessful approaches, such as ignoring the problem, telling everyone they had to learn to get along, and even moving the offices of the two people involved, along with others not directly involved, so they were not in the same area.

---

8   Daniel H. Pink, *Drive: The Surprising Truth about What Motivates Us* (New York: Riverhead Books, 2009).

Finally, they assigned a new manager to the department in the hopes that she would be able to provide a solution to the conflict that had eluded previous managers. The new manager wisely realized that she needed help to resolve the issue. She brought our company in to assist in resolving the conflict. We began by meeting with management and actively listening to gain an understanding of the conflict. We immediately perceived that, while this conflict was between two individuals, there were other problems that were feeding the ongoing tension. Some of the issues included:

- Lack of training for managers
- Delegation of responsibility without authority
- Management's unwillingness to address issues; their "Band-aid" approach to problems
- Perception of favoritism within the department

The good news is that, based on listening to the concerns, we were able to assist this organization in identifying the factors underlying the conflict and resolving them in a reasonable period of time. To resolve the issues, we provided training on how to adapt communication skills in order to be more effective. Staff was then given the opportunity to talk directly and openly about the issues, freeing them to voice their needs and work together toward a solution. We also worked with management, providing training on leadership and delegation skills.

The departmental manager reported later that things were going much better. They saw better cooperation from their team and productivity was on the rise, as was the number of new ideas the team was creating for improving their services. The executive team was also able to redirect their attention to other issues and needs, thus driving the organization forward.

This type of communication and collaboration allows team members to focus on solutions that are in the best interest of everyone involved, which are the only solutions that will truly succeed. On the other hand, if one party loses, the lingering tension will make it extremely difficult to succeed the next time they must work together to reach a goal. Passive-aggressive behavior erupts, and team members will begin presenting their arguments to others in an attempt to win support for "their side."

Another reason that leaders are reluctant to resolve conflicts is that they do not understand the goal of conflict resolution. Some leaders dislike the other party involved in the conflict, and therefore do not want to extend the energy needed to resolve the issue. A number of leaders we have worked with in resolving conflict will say, "That person is just too difficult to work with." But conflict resolution is not motivated by friendship. It is motivated by the potential achievements of a team. Nothing will kill your vision, mission, or opportunity for success like unresolved conflict. If you want others to respect your leadership, you cannot avoid the responsibility of resolving conflict quickly.

Assess Your Natural Leadership: Communication

1. How much time do you spend listening to your team?

2. Do you rely on the same communication styles and methods when you interact?

3. What percentage of the time are you telling your team what to do versus "selling" and engaging them in the process?

4. How often do you have to demand action and help from your team versus their freely offering to help?

Chapter 10:

Delegation and Empowerment

Adam stopped by a particularly dense area and began examining the plants along the path. "These all look so healthy. How does your team know how to care for all the different species?"

"To be sure, learning about all these different plants is one of our most challenging tasks," said Ned. "When I first started here, it was a bit overwhelming, even though I had a lot of experience caring for ecosystems. In fact, at first I thought I was the only one who could do most of the work, and so I gave only very basic tasks to the others."

"That must have been a relief for them not to have to work so hard," said Adam.

Ned smiled. "You would think so, but actually the team hated it. They felt I didn't have confidence in them. And they are very bright people. They knew they could accomplish the work if only I would give them a chance. I almost lost some of my best people."

View any ecosystem you find on two different dates, and you will see change. It is inherent to healthy organisms and ecosystems to grow and change. A plant will deepen its roots searching for nutrients, and as a result grow fuller and taller. An ecosystem will either grow or decline and ultimately die out. When a plant stops growing for a long time, its end is in sight. That said, many plants and trees need periods of rest or internal rejuvenation (e.g., certain trees drop their leaves in the fall) prior to outward growth.

Likewise, the same principles are true with your team. Leaders need to provide critical nutrients so their teams can grow and reach new horizons in their work. These nutrients include, among others, new responsibilities, learning opportunities, and the opportunity to try new ideas or approaches. When these are present, team members will stretch and grow in ways they have not in the past. They will be energized and fulfilled as never before, as they experience a feeling of ownership. They also need periods of rest, reflection, and rejuvenation to prepare for new growth. This can include times to get outside the office and experience new paradigms, attending conferences, and meeting with peers in the industry.

Many would suggest that delegation is just a way of getting something done. However, delegation is really about growing and empowering your team. When you look at the benefits to your team as well as to the organization, delegation becomes a powerful tool. Without delegation, growth for organizations and team members will be severely limited.

Maximizing creativity and ROI

One of the objectives of delegation is increasing staff ownership. Leaders must delegate not only tasks but also entire areas of responsibility to their team members. This does not come automatically to most leaders; many see delegation as a way to get tasks off their to-do lists quickly. But it is rarely appropriate to simply think of a particular task and ask a team member to complete it; such actions lack the scope to result in true ownership of that project or responsibility. Therefore, your staff member will complete the task and walk away, not thinking about the greater implications of his or her work, and certainly not thinking about revisiting this area of responsibility until the task is again due. Most tasks of this type are also routine and repetitive. Therefore, no real learning is happening; delegation simply gets a task completed for leaders. In contrast, true delegation should be focused on providing growth opportunities.

Another objective of delegation is to achieve the highest ROI (return on investment) with our staff. For instance, one of the biggest line-item expenses for many organizations is payroll costs, especially when combined with training, supervisory time, and other nonpayroll rewards. This investment fuels the growth of your company and so can be very valuable. However, if you have invested in a highly talented individual and then ask him or her to do mostly routine activity, reports, and administrative functions, your return is very low.

To obtain the highest ROI, each person must work at the peak of his or her capacity. This does not refer to quantity of work, although being efficient is always a good objective. Rather, this refers to the capacity to perform higher-impact tasks and responsibilities—those that will drive the organization forward and shape its future.

For example, with recent changes in technology, many business professionals are now expected to complete their own administrative work. This may appear to be a great cost-cutting process, freeing up dollars otherwise spent on administrative personnel. However, when you take a closer look at the results of this trend, you will find highly skilled professionals doing their own filing, typing correspondences, creating spreadsheets, and performing other administrative functions. While some of this may be appropriate, can you imagine the cost of having an executive who may be making $40 or $50 an hour typing their own correspondence?

Not only is the cost of this work too high, but it crowds out other high-impact work, reducing timeliness and quality. One of the most common complaints expressed by managers is that their days are full of meetings, reports, and other activities that keep them from the very responsibilities they were hired to fulfill. They get to the end of their week exhausted from the deluge of reports and frustrated because that project they desperately wanted to complete never got done.

Another objective of delegation is to create environments that are high in creativity and innovation. When we free people to work on high-impact activity, not only does their ROI increase, but so does their energy, engagement, and creativity. When staff members are given opportunities to learn and use their talents to the highest degree possible, it is highly motivating. Your most talented people will be drawn to this environment and will thrive, producing great advancements for your organization.

For example, Whirlpool understands this concept so well that they endeavor to move people into new positions of responsibility every two years. Employees gain new opportunities to learn, grow their skills, and avoid stagnating in their roles. However, to advance their careers, each professional is encouraged to look for a successor as they move into those new positions. This creates an opportunity for personal and professional growth, while the mentoring and mutual promotion creates an environment of cooperation and synergy. Why wouldn't talented people want to work in such a highly engaging environment?

You may be thinking that your organization is not large enough to move people into new roles every few years. However, a small organization can still achieve the same effect by assigning new responsibilities within a role. A team member's title does not need to change for them to learn new skills, apply new ideas, or take on new projects. Every team member should have a growth plan, whether or not they are seeking a new position within your organization.

For example, we were asked by a small company in the telecommunications industry to help them fill an administrative position. As we conducted interviews, one of the areas we explored was candidates' perception of the ideal supervisor. As we probed the relationship that candidates had with prior supervisors and why one supervisor was preferred over another, we found an interesting pattern. The best administrative candidates all said, "My previous supervisor would allow me to learn and take on new responsibilities. They were willing to give me a variety of tasks to complete and challenged me to grow."

This is what talented employees are seeking from your organization and from you as a leader. If you can learn to delegate, assist team members in growing, and then stay out of their way, your organization can achieve great things. You should be asking yourself and others some of the following questions:

- How can I be the best leader, the best receptionist, the best CFO that I can be?
- What shifts are taking place in the market and with our clients that necessitate change in how I am performing my tasks?
- In what way could I have a greater impact on my department or organization?

The answer to these questions will begin to reshape your role and the responsibilities of those on your team. Instead of looking at your responsibilities merely as a series of tasks that must be completed, you will begin to see the importance of initiating and stretching yourself beyond where you are today. Incorporating higher-priority activities into your schedule will necessitate delegating tasks you historically were involved in, providing growth for both you and your team. In fact, you will find your team taking greater ownership of their responsibilities as well.

Some team members enjoy routine work and want to stay in their current roles. They are not seeking a promotion or a whole new set of responsibilities. For them, delegation is still critical. No matter what the role, team members should be growing in their expertise and knowledge. If your receptionist wants to stay in that role, you should applaud that decision. However, the question still remains: how do you help him or her become the best receptionist he or she can be? What new things can he or she learn about your business that will allow him or her to effectively direct calls? Providing team members with new tasks can be a learning opportunity to excel right where they are.

Balancing freedom and boundaries

Effective delegation involves giving parameters for the team to work within, along with authority to act. Leaders must articulate the team's responsibilities, goals, creative parameters, and decision-making authority. If these are articulated well, leaders create an environment in which team members will grow and become highly productive.

Leaders must also resist the tendency to take projects back when things are not progressing as expected. This process requires leaders to focus on training and monitoring results, to ensure that teams are succeeding at tasks. If team members struggle in completing tasks, leaders can assist by providing additional training or resources.

However, they should not take the responsibility back, which would undermine the team's confidence and ability to learn from the experience. If full delegation fails to occur, the team will disengage and become passive. Leaders will not glean the best ideas or the strongest creativity from team members. Instead, leaders will spend their time putting out fires and making decisions for everyone on the team. In short, leaders will work far harder than if they were doing everything themselves and had no employees.

For example, a large company that was growing rapidly asked our firm to work with one of their management teams. This particular team oversaw one of the most promising service divisions in the organization. While the management team of this division was doing fairly well, the organization needed their team to act more independently and to create solutions instead of waiting for upper management. Most of their meetings revolved around problems that had arisen, with no solutions offered. Since there were so many issues on the agendas, meetings would go on for two to three hours with little resolution.

Therefore, we recommended that when the team came into the meeting, they present possible solutions. It was difficult at first, but soon the team learned the skill of making decisions and thinking through their recommendations. In the end, this saved the company and upper management untold time in meetings and lost productivity as people waited for management to solve their issues. It also resulted in better decisions, since this team knew firsthand both the issues and the possible solutions.

Delegation also requires that leaders are willing to allow team members to determine *how* they accomplish tasks or responsibilities. You may prefer certain work methods, but allowing your team members to determine their own methodologies within set parameters will create new and perhaps better ways of accomplishing the task. You may even find that once you see their ideas, you'll like them even better than the ones you've used for years. Staying open to fresh ideas and new ways of doing things is crucial for creating a highly productive environment.

In his book *The 21 Irrefutable Laws of Leadership,* John Maxwell states, "You have to give up, to move up." [9] The higher the level of leadership you hope to achieve, the greater the sacrifice. For example, leadership requires that you give up personal preferences and your control over every aspect of the operation. You must allow others to express their ideas and preferences, as long as it moves you toward the goal. Therefore your willingness to let go, delegate to others, and accept new ideas and approaches is key.

Many leaders and entrepreneurs have a tendency to micromanage. They are reluctant to let go of the task and let someone take ownership. This reluctance creates an environment in which staff members feel the need to check back with leaders for approval. Since they are not allowed to take risks, they will not grow or learn from their experiences.

Also, many leaders try to fix urgent problems quickly, instead of guiding the team in their pursuit of an answer. This creates dependency on leaders, rather than true learning and ownership.

---

9   John Maxwell, *The 21 Irrefutable Laws of Leadership* (Nashville: Thomas Nelson Publishers, 1998), 185.

For example, a business owner I worked with thrived on getting all the pieces in place and making sure that everything was being done perfectly. This desire to control and perfect every aspect of the business was creating an imbalance with the team, who couldn't perform their jobs or make decisions unless he was involved. Therefore, their growth was hindered and his team was dissatisfied with the work environment.

In working with him and conducting an organizational assessment, we uncovered the bottleneck that had resulted from his work style. We created checks and balances to ensure that the quality would continue, but without his involvement in each aspect of the business. As a result, staff members were free to be creative and make decisions about their work. Even the owner was much happier; with the additional time available to him, he began increasing his marketing efforts, and the company grew. His team also grew in their expertise and confidence in reaching new goals.

In delegating, leaders are also responsible for providing the needed tools and information for their teams. If team members do not understand the nature of the task, the history of what has happened before, the importance of the task, and its expected results, the process will fail. Nothing is more frustrating for your team than working diligently at a task, only to be told at the end that they did not reach your objective. All along they thought they were on the right track, only to realize that they lacked a piece of information necessary for success.

For example, a small sales organization once hired a salesperson to expand their market and obtain new clients. However, when the salesperson began, she received very little training, but rather was told to look through material and figure out what she needed to know. So the new salesperson began trying to identify clients based on where she had contacts and who she thought could use the company's product.

One day, the manager stopped the salesperson as she was about to leave and asked about where she was heading. Upon hearing that she was visiting a prospect in the biomedical industry, the manager reprimanded her. The manager felt that based on past experience, this industry was not a good market. This was frustrating for the salesperson, since she'd spent significant time trying to connect to prospects within that industry.

Without proper training and effective delegation, you can hinder your team's opportunity for growth and accomplishment. In this instance, no harm was done to the client, but the salesperson ended up discouraged and unwilling to initiate for fear the same thing would happen again. Fortunately, her manager realized that her training had been inadequate, and took the time to explain in greater detail the markets and industries that should be targeted. Therefore, the salesperson was able to regain confidence in her ability to achieve the objective.

Overcoming the temptation to do it all

One of the big challenges facing most leaders is an unspoken concern: if you give away some of your current responsibilities, what will you do with your time? And what value will you have within the organization if you are no longer doing things that seemed to have value in the past? The struggle for many leaders is that they base their value to the organization on how much they can personally accomplish. This is natural, since most people are promoted based on accomplishing a high number of tasks and getting things done on time. Promotions based simply on productivity have long sent the message that you get rewarded for being efficient and for personal accomplishment.

While these attributes are not bad, they are not the key to effective leadership. The key value for a leader is being able to produce *through others*. This requires us to be "effective" as well as efficient. Effectiveness for us as leaders refers to making strong decisions, empowering our team, motivating and persuading others, and multiplying our efforts through the team. These are very different skills and require time committed to these activities.

However, many leaders resist moving into these activities because they are more conceptual and harder to check off on a list. These objectives often do not have a clear start and end date, but rather are ongoing throughout the year. Therefore leaders often feel as if they have not accomplished as much at the end of the day, or the week, or the month.

Yet the reverse is actually true. As discussed earlier in the chapter, delegation actually has a greater impact in terms of ROI maximization and return for the organization than the traditional top-down view of management. Through delegation, you are multiplying your efforts and freeing team members to expand their capacity, which is essential for your organization to sustain growth.

A great exercise that I recommend to my clients is to pretend that you have to give away 50 percent of your responsibilities. Assume that you only have about twenty hours per week to devote to what you are currently doing. What would you give away? What activities and initiatives are so impactful to the future of your organization that you must keep them? The answer to these questions will begin to highlight which of your current tasks should be delegated to others.

Another obstacle for leaders is that, sometimes, you enjoy the activities that you know should be done by someone else. Just because we enjoy projects or tasks does not mean that it is appropriate for us to continue with them. If they do not sufficiently impact our organization, then we need to consider delegating them to others where the fit is appropriate. Consider the following: every time you do something that could or should be done by someone else, you are robbing them of the opportunity to grow. This thought changes our perspective and helps us see why it is so critical to delegate responsibility to others.

Some leaders do not delegate responsibility because they do not want to impose on their team. They work until 8:00 p.m. and allow their staff to leave at 5:00 or 5:30 p.m. Meanwhile, the team members wish they could expand their responsibilities and have a greater role in the success of the organization. Team members often will say that they would like to help shoulder the load and contribute on a higher level. However, they are often told by their leaders that there is nothing more the team can do, and that the leader is the only one who can accomplish certain critical tasks.

In effect, such leaders are saying they do not have confidence in the team and that they are the only ones capable of really important responsibilities. Delegating work is not an imposition, but rather an opportunity for growth and greater impact. It communicates confidence in your team and says that you value their abilities and contributions. When you reframe it in this way, the dangers of not delegating become all too evident.

Most leaders struggle with delegating, since it means letting go and allowing others to take on the areas they have held for so long. But while leaders can force others to agree with their preferences, in the end they lose a great deal. Their teams will resent their leadership, wait for specific direction, disengage from stretching to reach goals, and become apathetic.

This negativity will kill off the talented people; they will either leave for other, healthier environments, or they will slowly wither away.

Second, there are widespread, long-term consequences on morale when we fail to create positive, energized, synergistic environments. Recent studies have shown that approximately 60 percent of all Americans do not want to go to work and are not satisfied with their jobs. They show up to work physically but fail to produce what is needed for the economic health of their company or our country. This environment creates apathy, lack of ownership, and a tremendous number of people exiting corporate life.

The good news is that you as a leader can change that statistic. It will not cost more money and it will not take more time, just a different way of leading, a different focus of your time, and a desire to see your team reach new horizons. Leaders who are willing to let go of their "traditional" accomplishments will reap great rewards. Stop putting out fires, and begin delegating!

Assess Your Natural Leadership: Delegation

1. Have you created professional growth plans for your team?

2. When was the last time you praised members of your team?

3. Do you have benchmarks and strategies for each initiative your team is implementing?

4. How many new projects are designed by you? By others?

5. What is the ROI achieved in your personal work? In the work of your team?

Chapter 11:

Accountability

Adam and Ned continued on, and soon paused near some vines. "What about these?" asked Adam. "They can have a tendency to take over and dominate other plants. How do you prevent that?"

Ned pointed to a grating that Adam had not noticed before. "You see, we build in barriers to prevent that from happening. And we limit how many plants of this species we allow in the ecosystem. We know that, if left to itself, it could harm the other plants here. So we established boundaries and watch them carefully to ensure that these plants don't overrun them."

Every ecosystem has its own boundary or outer limits. Within the ecosystem, every component has a boundary in which it can thrive. For example, a river creates a boundary that nonaquatic animals would not be able to cross, and a desert creates a hot, barren boundary that would keep many animals from entering. These boundaries protect the ecosystem and allow it to grow in a healthy fashion. Boundaries are a critical part of nature's ability to grow and flourish. Without them, certain plants and animals would dominate and overpower others, thus creating shortages of certain elements essential for the health of the whole ecosystem. For example, many of the states bordered by the Great Lakes are looking for ways to prevent Asian carp from entering the lakes. If introduced into the lakes, they will probably dominate and kill off much of the other aquatic life. Therefore, caretakers of the environment must seek to support and maintain those natural boundaries.

Just as certain plants can invade a great ecosystem unless contained by natural barriers, so employees can destroy a corporate culture unless contained by accountability. Without accountability, chaos can ensue, as each person on the team performs in a manner that seems correct to him or her, but that in fact is not in harmony with the rest of the team. The result will be increased conflict, reduced productivity, and lack of progress.

One of the keys to creating a great environment is accountability. Providing guidelines and boundaries and monitoring results are critical ways in which leaders maintain healthy ecosystems. As a leader, you are responsible for creating opportunities for your team to take ownership, accomplish new goals, and grow. Through accountability, each individual can stretch and grow as they learn new skills, yet remain in harmony with the team.

Aiming for positive feedback

Creating accountability is one of the most valuable and yet most often avoided leadership activities. In many instances, leaders avoid it because they misunderstand what accountability actually involves. Many think it consists of correcting and disciplining employees for poor performance. They associate accountability and performance evaluations with unpleasant memories of being sent to the principal's office.

Instead, creating true accountability means focusing on reasons to praise your team. For instance, maybe your team has been working hard and persevering in the face of obstacles to reach important goals and objectives. To keep going, your team needs to receive a pat on the back and hear that you recognize what a great job they are doing. You don't have to wait for huge accomplishments; let them know you appreciate activities that matter and have importance to the team and the organization.

For example, at one time I provided leadership to four hundred volunteers. During the course of the year, I held volunteer recognition events and gave out holiday gifts. None of these gestures produced much feedback from our volunteers; the gifts were received pleasantly, but without much comment. In contrast, once a month I made sure that each volunteer received a handwritten note thanking them for their involvement and contributions. Invariably, I heard more feedback and appreciation for those handwritten notes than for anything else we did. It was a simple thing to send a handwritten note, but the impact was tremendous.

Many leaders feel that this act of giving praise is unnecessary. "After all," they say, "we pay them for their work. Isn't that enough? Why do we need to tell them they're doing a good job?" This reasoning is based on the assumptions that your team is able to read your mind (if you don't tell them differently, they should assume you're happy with their performance) and that money is their primary motivator. All of these assumptions are in fact false; in my own work, I've seen ample proof to the contrary. For example, as I've mentioned before, my firm typically asks candidates about why they've enjoyed working for their favorite past supervisors. In approximately 90 percent of the responses, the candidates indicated that they loved working for their favorite supervisor because of two things. The first thing they mentioned was that they were allowed to learn more and to stretch in their responsibilities. Secondly, they always knew where they stood and knew that their supervisor appreciated their efforts. In other words, they were held accountable for their work and received not only correction but also praise. Nothing is worse for employees than being blindsided during year-end performance evaluations, when they discover that their supervisor has been concerned about their performance for some time but never said anything about it to them. Accountability, then, is one of the most prized aspects of a supervisory relationship for many employees.

Creating accountability is not only about praising the team but also about looking for areas to build on. In other words, accountability provides you with the opportunity not only to evaluate how your team is doing but also to discern where you can be more effective in providing for their needs. For example, does the team need additional training? Do they need additional information to perform well and reach their goals? Do they need you to provide additional resources? It's critical as a leader to be aware of these needs; your job is to provide for and serve your team members.

For example, one supervisor in a human services agency made a point of regularly asking her team how the supervisor could improve. She would discuss the employees' work, how they were progressing toward their goals, and if there was anything the supervisor could do to support them in their efforts. This opened the door for the team members to give feedback about their needs and ways in which they could be more fully equipped. Just asking team members these questions created an open and honest environment that freed the team to perform and excel.

Talented staff will want to remain in such a relationship and environment. Talented people can earn money anywhere, but your openness to this type of dialogue cannot be replaced by money. Talented people are drawn to dynamic environments, opportunities that allow them to grow, and collaboration with other talented people. The benefit to you, of course, is that you retain the most talented people, which then allows you to grow in a highly competitive market.

Accountability is crucial in that it emphasizes what is important in each person's work. When you examine and provide feedback about someone's work, you are clearly denoting that what they are achieving is important. Everyone wants to know that they are valued and that they are contributing something important. By taking time to review their progress, you are demonstrating the value of their work. This process becomes a huge motivator for your team members as they press through difficult obstacles.

In contrast, I knew of a professional service organization that failed to follow through on their team's progress. First, they gave their team the assignment of developing goals for the year and plans for how they would achieve these goals. The first year this assignment was given, the organization's leaders gave the staff time during work hours to accomplish the plan and made themselves available if the team had any questions. The team was highly energized by the opportunity to create goals and plans. The team's report was turned in to management, and the team was praised for doing a good job.

However, as time went on, little more was said. When benchmarks were missed, the team was told that they just needed to work smarter, not harder. No other tools or ideas were furnished about how to improve their work so they could reach their goals. In fact, during the second half of the year, the goals were not even reviewed. This sent a message to the team that management did not consider the goals or missed opportunities to be important.

The second year, management came back with the same request for staff to put together another set of goals and plans. This time, however, the team was told that they would only be allowed to work on the plan outside of office hours. This also meant that management was not available to answer questions or offer suggestions during their discussions. Therefore, the team met to work on the plan, but energy and enthusiasm were low. The team recalled how little impact the plan had the year before, and so they simply made minor revisions to the previous year's plan and turned it in to management. Management gave no feedback on the plan, and it was placed in a file somewhere, not to be seen again for the entire year.

In effect, the staff's suspicion that their work made little difference was confirmed when management failed to provide feedback, either positive or negative, about their work. Management did not intend to demoralize and frustrate their team, but failure to provide accountability had just that effect. Morale continued to decline, and staff began going through the motions instead of bringing their best effort to their work. What a loss, when the team had started out the process with such positive energy!

If leaders are not willing to invest in providing accountability, their teams will not invest in the activities and projects assigned to them. Instead, apathy will rise and productivity will drop as employees discover that missed goals have no impact.

Finally, accountability is about proactively identifying threats to your projects and ensuring that timelines are being met. After all, if there is an obstacle looming in the distance, you want to know as soon as possible to allow for effective problem solving. Such accountability is the joint responsibility of leaders and team members. They work in tandem to ensure that they are identifying threats to the project. For example, if one person in a team falls behind, the others will be impacted as well, so there's a joint responsibility to correct that person's progress. Therefore, setting benchmarks throughout a project and monitoring them for progress allows you and the team to avoid missed opportunities.

This proactive process allows team members to focus on their priorities and solve problems early on in the process. Without accountability, problems are usually identified late in the process, and then management is required to quickly step in to fix the problem. Your team will then come to rely on you for answers rather than taking ownership of the issues and the solutions to those obstacles.

Going beyond the year-end evaluation

Many leaders immediately think of performance reviews when the subject of accountability is raised. While year-end reviews provide in-depth opportunities for evaluation and accountability, they should not be the only time we engage in these activities. For instance, if your team members are struggling with project management, do you really want to wait until a formal performance evaluation to help them correct their actions? By that time, you will have lost the majority of the year to poor productivity, when you could have greatly strengthened their performance if you'd addressed it properly.

Instead, accountability should be provided both informally, as an ongoing process, and formally (ideally, two to four times a year). When you observe behaviors that deserve either praise or correction, provide it immediately. Being alert to the efforts of your team will allow you to reinforce and reward their progress. Informal accountability also lets your team members know that you are serious about issues that have been addressed, and that you are watching to ensure that correction will begin right away.

Formal accountability, as provided by a full performance appraisal, should occur at least two to four times a year. Through multiple meetings, you can reinforce team members' goals, give broad feedback about their performance, and gain feedback from them about how things are going. Therefore, it is important to meet formally and discuss their performance. This also allows you to understand their perspective in terms of their needs for support, communication, training, and resources.

Some leaders struggle to conduct an evaluation process even once a year and therefore resist the idea of doing this more often. These same leaders often share their frustrations about having to put out fires, redirect team members, and confront staff about missed deadlines. Why? Because their communication and reinforcement of priorities was lacking until it was too late to resolve the issues.

Instead, by meeting more frequently and doing an abbreviated midyear evaluation, you can assist in refocusing efforts, reminding staff of priorities, and providing needed correction when there is still time to succeed. Your staff will appreciate the endeavor to support their efforts and realize that you are invested in their work. The dividends are huge, not to mention the fact that you will enjoy your work much more as well.

Another benefit of this regular process is that it will prevent your team from just going through the motions without thinking about how they could improve. Accountability produces growth in each team member, as they stretch to learn and achieve new things. When team members are questioned about their progress and growth, they'll be guided to think about what else they need to achieve and how they can fulfill their responsibilities in a better fashion. In effect, accountability sharpens their thought process and skills. Therefore, accountability will inevitably lead to growth for the individual and the organization.

Providing blameless and tailored evaluations

However, to achieve benefits from accountability, you must learn to provide it in a skillful fashion. Most of us have seen the destructive nature of poorly provided accountability. Staff morale goes down, people stop taking initiative, and staff members become resentful and defensive. Staff members become critical of others and may feel the need to point out others' flaws to make themselves look better.

In contrast, strong, positive accountability rests on two things: respectful, blameless assessment and tailored communication. First, you must communicate respectfully about the areas that need to be changed and strengthened. Rather than demeaning people and making them feel as if they have failed, focus on solutions to preventing a reoccurrence. You and your team understand that a mistake was made, but dwelling on that mistake will not help you move forward; it will only create an environment in which people are afraid to risk failure. Leaders must encourage and provide opportunities for staff to try new ideas, risk new projects, and make bold decisions without fear of blame. By allowing people to learn, we will bring energy and passion to our organizations. Our teams will thrive, grow, and take on additional responsibilities if given constructive feedback that respects their contribution and attempts.

Of course, you do not want errors to be repeated. But making mistakes is part of the learning process. Out of the mistakes we make, we learn important truths that assist us in moving forward. For example, did Thomas Edison invent the light bulb correctly on the first try? Did Abraham Lincoln get elected to every political office for which he ran? These were bright people who could have given up and said that they couldn't succeed because they experienced a setback. However, through their mistakes they learned valuable information that helped them to come closer to the right answer the next time. These repeated attempts ultimately led to success. When you regularly review and communicate how team members are doing, they will similarly find success.

Second, leaders must consider team member's styles when providing accountability. Each member will be impacted differently by your words of praise and correction. For instance, some people enjoy the limelight and prefer to have praise given publicly. For them, being mentioned in front of others means far more than a note left on their desk. For others, being praised in front of a group would be extremely embarrassing. They would rather have you praise them in private or leave a note for them to read on their own.

Furthermore, some people are fine with a general note of praise, such as "You're doing a great job." For others, that praise would be meaningless; they'd need to hear, "You did such a great job on choosing colorful decorations that match our company colors for our staff party." In other words, one size does not fit all.

When you provide correction, you must consider the impact you will have. For instance, if you are too direct with some individuals, they will withdraw and give up. You will crush their spirit and initiative and cause them to lose confidence in their abilities. On the other hand, there are some who need and want a very direct approach in sharing feedback.

The key in both of these examples is to ask what will produce the best results. The answer to this question does not lie with your personal preferences, but rather with the individual's personal preferences and needs. This process of selecting the best tool and method to bring about awareness and change is critical. Too many times, leaders approach a team member in the wrong way and cause far more damage than good. When something seems natural to us, we struggle to understand why it wouldn't be preferred by others.

If you study behavioral styles through DISC, or any other behavioral system, you will begin to understand how differently each person desires to be approached. These differences affect their interests, communication styles, how they use their time, and how they prefer to interact with you. Effective leaders will become adept at changing their approach to match that of the individual with whom they are talking.

This ability to adapt to others' preferences is essential for leaders who truly desire to impact the team. It demonstrates respect for the individual; it allows the person to hear and benefit from your input; it creates strong trust and relationships between you and your team members; and it can result in multiple benefits for the team. This is critical for you as you seek to impact your team and access the benefits we discussed earlier in this chapter.

Assess Your Natural Leadership: Accountability

1. How often do you review your team member's progress?

2. Is your performance review primarily focused on things that need improvement or on what they are doing well?

3. What resources and efforts are directed toward staff growth?

4. Do you evaluate your team's attitudes, teamwork, and values as well as their job performance?

5. How effective are you at turning mistakes into teachable moments and learning opportunities?

Conclusion:

The Choice Is Yours

When it comes to current crises in the natural environment, there are basically three types of responses. One response is that, while you know that you're leaving a huge carbon footprint, you do not really care. You continue your day-to-day practices with little regard for the negative impact you are having on the environment. Your focus and concern are on your needs, desires, and preferences.

Similarly, in the corporate world, we see leaders whose attention tends to be on the here and now, not on how their actions will impact the long term. Therefore, they think resources are to be used at will, in any way that fits their purposes at the moment. They are reactive in nature, rather than proactively preparing for the future. Some of them will even manipulate and use people and their strengths for their own advantage in the short term. They don't worry about losing clients or talented employees. Their focus is on getting sales in the door now. They are leaving huge footprints of negativity, fear, and destruction within the organization.

To continue with our analogy, another type of response to environmental crises is tokenism. You *say* you care about your negative impact on the environment and will do something to change the impact as long as the cost is not too high. Examples of this might be people who will change the light bulbs in their homes or recycle their newspapers. They are willing to make a start in the right direction, but beyond a certain point, their willingness to change dwindles. Look at the large number of SUVs on the road or how few people carpool or use mass transit, and you begin to see how large the problem actually is in our country.

Likewise, some corporate leaders *say* they are committed to their employees, but they do not want to be inconvenienced too much by others' needs. On an intellectual basis, they choose to "try" to do what is right. They provide a basic form of health care, or give staff members a bonus at the end of the year, but invest very little in their development or learning about their aspirations. At some level they do care, but they spend limited time or energy to act on their concern. They do little to help their staff members to thrive, and investing in their team is not a high priority.

The third response to crises in the natural world is true environmentalism. Committed environmentalists embrace the truth of their actions' consequences and take active steps to change. They look for ways to improve themselves and minimize their environmental impact. They evaluate their daily behaviors and habits to identify where they can change so as to have a positive impact on the environment. They go beyond intellectual commitment and take action whenever possible. They sacrifice some preferences, comforts, conveniences, and costs, and passionately seek the best environmental solutions available.

In a similar fashion, natural leaders have a continuous impact on the culture and environment in which their teams operate. They are committed to the activities, decisions, and strategies that will cause their teams to thrive. They are not satisfied with an environment in which people just survive. They understand that people are complex and have greater needs than salaries and benefits. These leaders see their role as one of service.

But why would a leader make this commitment? It certainly does not seem at first glance to add to the bottom line. It requires more work, effort, and commitment on the part of leaders. Further, it's not even expected by most boards of directors, who are mainly observing the financial health of an organization.

The rationale for this commitment comes on several levels. First of all, it's the right thing to do. People contribute a major portion of their lives to their employers. Studies have shown that the paycheck is not a true compensation for that commitment; it may cause employees to show up every day, but high productivity only comes when employees are motivated, engaged, and passionate about what they are creating.

Second, there are long-term consequences when we fail to create positive, energized, synergistic workplaces. As stated before, recent studies have shown that approximately 60 percent of all Americans do not want to go to work and are not satisfied with their jobs. They show up to work physically but fail to produce what is needed for the economic health of their company or our country. This environment creates apathy, a lack of ownership, and a tremendous number of people exiting corporate life.

Third, making a commitment to a healthy corporate environment is critical because without it, we cannot sustain growth and profitability. You may gain short-term growth, but you will never be able to sustain that growth without creating the type of "natural" environment we are describing. If a team lacks engagement in or ownership of their service or product, they will not commit the energy and creativity to push through obstacles. They will not provide the needed solutions to succeeding consistently.

The next chapter in our story is yours to write. The world, or at least your corner of the world, is in your hands. What will you do with that corner of the world? Your organization, team, and clients are looking for natural leaders who will step up and create (as well as protect) an incredible environment for them—leaders who will serve the good of those they lead. People follow leaders who reflect their values and invest in the most sustainable and impactful goals.

There are many smart and talented people. However, the impact of a person's leadership is not based on raw talent or intelligence. Those help, to be sure, but the real measure of a person's leadership is how he or she uses his or her abilities for the greater good. Are they natural leaders who passionately create vision, inspire a team, and serve the interests of their clients? Natural leaders are not born; instead, they're people who determine within themselves to be about something bigger, better, and greater than their counterparts. They are about creating a better world, a better organization, and a better team. They are natural leaders. Commit to implementing the steps needed to strengthen your leadership skills. Now is the time to act!